FIRE
ICE
AIR

A Polish Jew's Memoir of Yeshiva, Siberia, America

RABBI SIMCHA SHAFRAN
with Avi Shafran

Hashgacha Press
12 Roanoke Street
Staten Island, NY 10314

ISBN-13: 978-0615598192
ISBN-10: 0615598196

Cover Design: Esther Freedman, Effective Designer

Communications:

Rabbi Simcha Shafran
3008 Lightfoot Drive
Pikesville, MD 21208

Fax: 410 484-1082

E-mail: hashgachapress@gmail.com

Foreword

Rabbi Simcha Shafran

Every survivor of the Shoah has stories to tell. And every perceptive survivor recognizes the hand of G-d, the *hashgacha p'ratis*, or "personalized concern," that guided him to survival.

But not every survivor speaks of his experiences, for different reasons.

Some, because to tell what happened is to relive it.

Some, because they want to forget.

And some feel guilty for surviving when other greater and more worthy Jews did not.

The question of those feelings of guilt is not an easy one to address.

My small glimpse of an approach is that there are different degrees of danger. When a person is in a place of special peril, the Talmud states, even great merits may not be enough to save him, to cause actual miracles to be performed on his behalf. And so there were times and places where even the best perished. "Once permission is given the destroyer to destroy," say the Rabbis, "it makes no distinction between the righteous and the wicked" (Bava Kama 60a).

Even the prophet Samuel, the Talmud relates, feared that King Saul might kill him if he confronted him as he had been commanded to do (Pesachim 8b). Despite the prophet's merits, the danger was just too great.

And, on the other hand, a person who doesn't necessarily have great merits but who finds himself in less dangerous situations — even during the same era when righteous are perishing — might survive. We survivors have no way of knowing the degrees of the dangers each of us was actually in over the years of the Second World War.

And then, of course, there are the merits that are not our own that can still protect us: the merits of our parents or grandparents, or more distant ancestors.

So we survivors can wonder, and we should be very thankful. But we should not feel guilty.

I was urged by my family to record the happenings of my life during and after the war. With my son Avi's help, I have tried to recall as many situations as I could. Many things, unfortunately, have been erased or blurred beyond recollection.

But I hope that what I have been able to remember, this story of a 14-year-old boy all on his own at the beginning of a terrible time in history – and his experiences over the years that, thank G-d, have followed – might help inspire readers to realize the importance of *bitochon*, or trust, in G-d, and help them resolve to live proper Jewish lives, as servants of the Creator.

Where can I depart from Your spirit?
And where can I fly from Your presence?
If I ascend to the heavens, You are there
If I lie in the depths, behold! – it is You.
Were I to rise with wings of dawn,
or to dwell at the distant sea
There, too, Your hand would guide me
And Your right hand hold me firm.

TEHILLIM (PSALMS) 139:7

Introduction

Avi Shafran

I had the happiest of childhoods.

It never occurred to me when I was young that my parents had experienced anything other than the same.

I didn't know until many years later that my mother, of blessed memory, had been transplanted to the United States from Poland as a very young girl, that, at 14, she had lost her grandmother, the only grandparent who had been part of her life, and then, mere weeks later, her 20-year old brother, who had been studying in yeshiva in New York. Two years later, her father passed away as well. I didn't know that she, as a teenager, had come to conclude that sitting *shiva*, the week-long mourning period for a close relative, was just part of the Jewish year-cycle.

Any scars she bore were invisible. She was the most normal, caring mother one could imagine and, as the local Rebbetzin, or rabbi's wife, she was beloved for her empathy and kindness, not only by my sister and brother and me but by the members of the synagogue my father served, by their children, to whom she gave special attention, and by all who knew her.

Now, twenty years since her passing, I miss her every single day.

As I do her mother, who lived with us for many years before her own passing, who didn't allow her personal losses to in any way affect her regal dignity and loving nature, and who was a vital part of my upbringing.

Nor did it occur to me that my father, may he live and be well, was anything other than a typical hard-working, caring Jewish father, the kind who sets a sterling example for his children, who teaches them how to study Torah, how to ride a bike, how to live.

I remember how, as a little boy, I would explode with joy when he would return home from the synagogue on Friday nights, interrupting my elaborate living-room floor war games, abandoning the scores of little grey plastic Confederate soldiers I had carefully arrayed against their blue Union counterparts.

When that door opened, the Civil War abruptly ended. Tata was home and it was time to sit at the luminous Sabbath table, to sing Shalom Aleichem, hear Kiddush, or the sanctification of the day, eat the special meal that had beckoned in my mind's eye and mind's stomach over the eternity of the previous six days.

No, as a child I never had a clue about the depth of poverty in which my father had spent his childhood, and certainly not about his family's displacement from their Polish *shtetl* by the Second World War. I was not aware of how he had left his parents and siblings mere weeks into the war, about his journey to Lithuania to study in yeshiva or his banishment to Siberia.

I knew nothing of those things alone, much less anything of their details.

Which means, of course, that my parents hadn't spoken to my brother, sister and me about their pasts.

I think my mother had consciously decided not to share with us the story of her early life, out of a desire to not allow the tragedy and mourning that had interrupted her childhood to have any presence – even in mere consciousness – in ours.

And my father, may he be well, for his part, I think, simply didn't want to confront the pain of memory.

When I was 14 or 15, I came to realize at least the basic story line of my parents' respective youths. In the case of my father, that general realization congealed into a tangible reality suddenly one night, and fell on me like a concrete block.

We had a television in those days, a medium that had not yet settled into its current place in the mire that is contemporary popular culture. My epiphany, ironically, was provoked by that rabbit-eared box, in the form of a documentary about the Holocaust, narrated by the actor Richard Basehart. That I remember such a detail is testimony to how deeply the program affected me.

I think I had certainly seen photographs of concentration camp carnage before, but somehow, the camera's panning over mounds upon mounds of tangled limbs barely yet immediately recognizable as human beings forced a thought: That arm could be my grandfather's; that head, my grandmother's; that leg, my uncle's; that pale, emaciated torso, my cousin's.

From then on, I began to think in an entirely new way. I found myself comparing where I was at stages in my life – what I was doing, the challenges I was facing, my achievements, hopes and goals – with where my father had been at those same stages of his life.

Needless to say, the contrasts were, to understate it, formidable.

Where I was trying to avoid boring teachers, he was fleeing Nazis; where my religious dedication consisted of getting out of bed early in the morning to attend services, his entailed leaving his parents at the start of a war to go study in a yeshiva; where I struggled to survive the emotional strains of teenage peer-relationships, he was struggling to survive in Siberia.

Over ensuing years I occasionally asked my father about his past. He wasn't anxious to share the details of his experiences, but obliged – to a degree – all the same.

It wasn't, though, until I was an adult, and not a particularly young one at that, that I first heard my father relate that for years after the war's end, when he took a shower he thought of the likely fate of his parents; and that, as my mother recalled, he would regularly startle her in the early years of their marriage by waking up suddenly in the middle of the night from a nightmare that had transferred him back across the Atlantic Ocean.

When, in the 1990s, I became aware of the Shoah Foundation's oral history project, the brainchild (and generously supported child) of the director Steven Spielberg, I asked my father to allow himself to be interviewed as part of that effort.

He resisted. He did not see what purpose it would serve. I persisted, though, and eventually he relented. Any regrets I may have felt about pestering my father to undergo the interview disappeared when I spoke to him afterwards. He seemed happy to have had his recollections recorded for posterity – and, viewing the videotape, I learned things – many things – that I had never known about my father's life.

It was only several years later that it occurred to me to turn my father's memories into a written and more ordered, comprehensive memoir.

This book is the realization of that idea. I took my father's words as conveyed to the Shoah Foundation interviewer, Ilene Kenney, and followed up with interviews of my own to further explore areas left uncharted by the video interview.

I gleaned information, too, from an article by the late Reb Chaim Shapiro, of blessed memory (who had been a dear friend of my father), "The World of

Novardok," published in *The Jewish Observer* in 1977. And much, too, from an impressive Hebrew work, *Lev Ha'ari*, that tells the story and presents thoughts of Rabbi Yehudah Leib Nekritz, of blessed memory, who headed the Novardhok Yeshiva during its final days in Lithuania, and who served as the spiritual mentor and leader of the small band of young men, my father among them, who persevered for four years in the wilderness of Siberian exile.

To the author and compiler of that latter work, Rabbi Doniel Nekritz, I offer my deep appreciation for his permission to include a number of facts and passages from it. And my indebtedness is great, too, to my esteemed friend Rabbi Hillel Goldberg, who is a font of information about Novardhok; to Mr. Spielberg, for his recognition of the importance of recording survivors' histories and his determination to make it happen; to Ms. Kenney, for her interview; to the Baltimore Jewish Times, for its permission to include material from its pages; to Chaya Sara Stern, for creating a transcript of the interview and assisting with photographs; to David Gerstman; to Jeremy Staiman; and especially to my daughter Esther Freedman, who designed this book's cover and the photograph pages.

My thanks are due as well to my sister and brother, Mrs. Rochel Zoberman and Rabbi Noach Shafran, and to others — some whose names appear in this book but others whose names do not but who nevertheless provided information and memories. And above all, my heartfelt gratitude goes out to my wife Gita, for her top-notch proofreading, suggestions and, well, everything.

The story herein is for the most part recounted chronologically and likewise for the most part in my father's voice. There are, though, occasional interjections from other times and recollections of other people (myself included), each italicized, framed and, when possible, duly dated. And later chapters include reminiscences of others that are intended to complement and illuminate my father's first-person memoir. He is willing to recall what happened to him but shies away from recounting what he has accomplished. So that is delivered here largely in the words of others.

Many details of the war years, my father says, are no longer available to his memory — more than sixty years' passage will do that. He is a stickler for honesty and will not supply any "information" that is speculative rather than strictly factual. Emulating him, I have resisted the urge to imagine events, scenes or dialogue. That may limit the book in some ways; I hope it strengthens it in other, more important, ones.

The "fire" of this book's title refers to the conflagration that consumed the world of my father's childhood, and to the fire that was the Torah-study of Novardhok; the "ice," to his Siberian sojourn. "Air" is the freedom he found upon his arrival on American shores, the atmosphere in which he raised his family, and taught and guided – and, thank G-d, continues to – so many others.

My father is a powerful part of his children's lives, of course, and of those of his grandchildren and great-grandchildren, may he and his wife, our dear "Bobby Ethel," merit to see many more. In his modest, quiet way, through his service as a rabbi in Baltimore for more than a half-century and in his current role as *mazkir*, or administrator, of the city's Orthodox Jewish religious court, the Baltimore Beis Din, my father has become part of the lives of yet countless others.

Now, dear reader, if you choose to read on, he will become part of yours too.

I lift up my eyes to the mountains

PSALMS, 121

✡ ✡ ✡

Said Rabbi Shimon bar Nachmeni: "Read the word not as 'mountains'
(harim), but rather as 'parents' (horim)"

YALKUT SHIMONI, 871

PART I

Home, and Leaving It

Second week of October, 1939 (end of Tishrei, 5700)

I realize now, 70 years later, how reasonable my parents were that autumn day, and how irrational and stubborn I was.

I cannot imagine what made me so determined to board that train and go off to yeshiva. I was 14 years old and had with me only the clothes I was wearing, my tefillin (the leather boxes and straps that a Jewish male is required to don daily) and a few apples my mother had given me. How had I managed to convince my parents to let me leave them and go my own way — a mere month after the outbreak of the Second World War, after we had been forced to flee our town and were almost burned alive?

Whatever it was that pushed me, it was the last time I would see my mother and father, and it was my refusal to be sensible that saved my life.

A HOUSE IN A TOWN
ON THE NAREV

Childhoods leave both bitter and sweet memories, and mine is no exception. Although there were many Jews in our town, Ruzhan, in northeastern Poland, many non-Jews lived there as well. They did not much care for us Jews.

Which was why I stopped attending the local school. One of my earliest memories is of an older non-Jewish boy walking up to me without reason or warning and punching me in the face. He ran away after the blow and, although I was only seven or eight, I chased him, wanting to even the score. I have never liked owing anybody anything, and here was an unpaid debt I wanted to set straight.

We ran alongside a river and he grew smaller before my eyes. When I realized that I had no hope of overtaking him, I just stopped running and cried.

When things like that happened, and they often did, we sometimes heard the taunt *"Zhidi Yitchi da Palistinya !"* – "Jews, go to Palestine!" My parents would have loved to do just that, had only they been able to. Two of my older brothers had managed to leave Poland illegally and settle in Palestine, but the rest of our family remained mired in the land of our birth, a motherland with less than maternal feelings for some of its children.

When Pesach, or Passover, approached, my parents would tell us children to stay indoors. Sermons in the churches that time of year, spring, spurred our Gentile neighbors to try to kill Jews. The churchgoers would parade around wearing big black hats, holding flags with religious symbols and figures painted on them. We used to peek through the window to take in the sight. But we never ventured out of doors when the townsfolk were marching.

And yet, a child is still a child, and the hatred our neighbors felt for us Jews became just part of the background noise of my life. There were games to play, there was fun to be had.

Not much, of course. But I remember rolling the rim of a bicycle tire down the road, using a stick to keep it upright and rolling. And watching the crystalline patterns formed by the ice on the inside of the window in the winter, and the play of the Chanukah candles upon them.

Although my father, Reb Avrohom Yitzchak Szafranowicz, was a simple Jew, a cabinetmaker by profession, he was a religious man, respected in the community and a regular in the synagogue. As for me, my aspiration was to be a rabbi one day.

I remember once being laid up in bed with a bad sore throat. For several days, I didn't go to the *cheder*, the one-room Jewish school where the town's Jewish children were taught the basics of Hebrew and Torah. I lay there under a blanket, with the accepted medical treatment, a stocking filled with hot ashes, tight against my neck.

The morning I began to feel a bit better, I took my blanket, put it up over my head like a prayer shawl and delivered my very first sermon to an invisible congregation. I even remember its subject, the song our ancestors sang after emerging from the sea G-d had parted for them to escape their Egyptian pursuers. The message of my sermon was straightforward, and it was one that, in the years that would follow, I came to know well in a most personal way: G-d makes miracles.

Our town was atop a hill, and in its center was a marketplace, which featured a water pump for the townsfolk's use, and the synagogue. I remember taking my aged and blind maternal grandfather, Yaakov Gelchinsky, to the synagogue. He had built the house in which we lived.

One of the streets leading from the marketplace winded down the hill toward the river Narev. The town *mikveh*, or Jewish ritual bath, was halfway down the hill. We lived at its bottom. When spring arrived and the ice and snow melted, the river swelled and came up to our doorstep.

For a short period of time, I attended public school. I think I was the only Jewish boy in the school, and one day, for one or another transgression, the teacher asked me to stretch out my hand in front of him. I did and he quickly brought the large, heavy ruler he was holding down hard on my hand, which burned with pain for days afterward. After that, I refused to go back to the school.

The poverty was powerful. Children were happy to get a piece of bread (especially with sugar atop it, and on rare occasions even butter), overjoyed at a pair of shoes. I remember crying bitterly one morning shortly before Pesach because I so wanted a new pair of shoes like some other boys had. My shoes were hand-me-downs several times over, and were both ill-fitting and ragged. But my parents had no money.

So I cried. But then, unexpectedly, some money came through the mail from Nachman, one of my two brothers who had made their way to Palestine. It was one of G-d's miracles. I received a new pair of shoes

When vegetables were available, in the summer, my father would buy heads of cabbage, which my mother would slice and put into a barrel to ferment. The resulting sauerkraut would be a staple at our table throughout the winter. Before Pesach, she would make noodles out of only eggs and potato starch. In our soup, they were a taste of heaven.

Our kitchen had a dirt floor. My younger brother Menachem and I used to take a bucket and shovel to a large hill of yellow sand and bring a bucketful of it home to neatly spread over the floor in honor of Shabbos, the Sabbath.

Shabbos in our home, as in every observant Jewish home, was a radiant time. A special stew – *cholent* – would be eaten at the Sabbath day meal. But the *cholent* had to be placed on a fire on Friday, before the arrival of the Sabbath, and to cook until the following afternoon. Since few homes could afford to keep a fire going, a local bakery would heat up its large oven before Shabbos, and many families, including ours, would bring their *cholent* to the bakery, leaving it in its oven overnight. On Shabbos morning, children from each of the families would be sent to retrieve their *cholent*s. Usually they found the right pot, but sometimes there were mixups, and families would be treated to a *cholent* made a bit differently from their own.

Menachem and I were our family's *cholent*-fetchers. I remember our trips up the hill to the bakery and how we would return, beaming, with the steaming pot.

Another Sabbath delicacy was *challah*, the braided bread baked especially for the day. And then there was the delicious fish. That dish was delectable to me, maybe made more so by what I had to endure to get it to the table. We had no way of refrigerating perishables, of course, and fish, especially in the summer, didn't keep very long. But we had a basement — so to speak. It was really just a large hole in the ground, accessible by a ladder. But it was naturally cold down there, even in the summer, and so we would put food that needed to be kept cold in the dark underground room – in a pot with a heavy rock on top of it, to frustrate the rats.

I would be sent down to the cellar to bring up the pot of fish, and was always terrified to make the short trip. I descended into the dark unknown as quickly as I could, and came up even quicker. But then it all became worth it, as our family sat and ate the heavenly fish, singing Sabbath songs. On Shabbos, we were kings of the world.

Second week of October, 1939 (end of Tishrei, 5700)

My mother kissed me goodbye, and I kissed her back. I boarded the train and as it began to travel, she receded slowly and then disappeared.

A few minutes later, though, looking out the window, I saw a truck carrying a group of men — among them was my older brother Fischel! I don't know where he was coming from, but he was heading back to my parents. He saw me through the window and waved to me. I wasn't able to speak to him, and in fact never would again. I waved back.

CHEDER DAYS

had seven brothers and sisters. My oldest sister Freida Leah was married and lived in a nearby town. Chaim Meir and Nachman were in Eretz Yisrael, or Palestine. At home were Fischel, eight or nine years older than I; my sisters Tzirel and Golda and my younger brother Menachem. Fishel always took an interest in what I was studying, encouraging me to be a good student. He also cared for me and entertained me.

Once he heated a wire and somehow used it to remove the bottom of a bottle, and then took a tin cover of a used-up shoe polish container and melted a candle to its middle. Then he put the bottle over the tin cover and candle and attached the two. Finally, tying three strings to the contraption, he presented me with a lantern to use to light my way coming home from *cheder* at night.

Since I had to pass a yard where a vicious dog snarled at me and strained against a chain that always seemed (at least to my imagination) ready to break, the lantern helped me see in front of me and allowed me to hurry my steps. To this day when I see a large dog, I feel an echo of the fear that would seize me each day on the way to and back from *cheder*.

In time, I was sent to a nearby town, Ostrolenka, where my father's father was a rebbe, or Jewish educator. My grandfather, who at that point had already retired from the classroom, was nevertheless still known as Reb Lazer Elya Der Melamed, or "Rabbi Eliezer Eliyahu the Teacher."

I spent a few weeks with him when I was about nine, and then returned home. About a year later, I returned to my grandfather's house and attended a branch of the famed Bais Yosef — or Novardhok — yeshiva in his town.

My grandmother had drowned one winter when she ventured onto a frozen pond to fetch water and the ice gave way. My grandfather and his second wife were very kind to me but very poor, and so I was their guest only on the Sabbath.

During the week, I would eat my meals, like many of the students, at the homes of townsfolk, a different home each day. The days I was placed in the local baker's home were the best, as the bread was plentiful and fresh. When I ate at a home where the food did not seem appetizing to me, not wanting to offend my hosts by leaving it on my plate, I would quietly put it in my pocket when no one was looking.

My grandfather and his wife were not the poorest people in the town. I would see kind people walk from house to house on Friday afternoons collecting pieces of *challah* for those who did not have even that simple staple.

I became Bar Mitzvah in Ostrolenka. My parents had no money to make the trip. I read from the Torah and recited the *haftarah*, the reading from the Prophets; and, a month earlier, began donning *tefillin*. My grandfather brought a little bottle of whiskey to the synagogue that morning, along with a few *kichel*, hollow cookies, and that was my Bar Mitzvah celebration.

September 1, 1939 (17 Elul, 5699)

A WORLD INTERRUPTED

I was supposed to travel to Bialystok in the fall of 1939, to attend the higher-level Novardhok Yeshiva there, and I had returned home to see my parents before going off to that place of higher Jewish learning. On September 1, 1939, however, my plans, like so many people's, were interrupted by the Second World War. The Nazis invaded Poland and we were told to expect bombing. I remember how, that Friday afternoon, people taped over their windows so that any glass that broke wouldn't shatter and hit those inside the houses. We listened to a radio until the Sabbath arrived.

Early the next morning, a neighbor knocked loudly on the door and told us breathlessly that the Germans had crossed the border and were not far from our town, and that we had to run away. The assumption was that Polish forces would soon destroy the bridge over the Narev, to prevent the Germans from advancing so quickly. If we were to stay ahead of the Germans ourselves, we had to cross the bridge first.

So, although travel outside of a city or town is not usually permitted on the Sabbath, the rabbi of the town rendered his decision that we were all in mortal danger and that it was thus not just permitted but required of us to flee.

As we lived near the river, we walked along its banks toward the bridge. We were told that in the event that a German airplane might drop a gas bomb on us we should run to the river, wet cloths and put them over our mouths and noses. At one point a plane did appear overhead. There was some panic but nothing fell from the sky.

Throngs of people were already at the bridge when we arrived there, but we all managed to cross over to the other side. We walked to Govrov, a nearby town with a Jewish community.

My parents, and all the new refugees, were frightened, with no idea what the future would bring. We were taken in by the locals in Govrov and remained there until the next Thursday. That was when we heard cannon fire from the direction from which we had come. Although Polish soldiers had remained on the Ruzhan side of the bridge, it was clear that they had not successfully stymied the Germans, and that the Nazis were advancing.

That night, several families, ours among them, set off again, and walked through the night. I took my *tefillin*, which were in a bag that closed with a drawstring, and hung them on my belt, to make sure that, whatever happened to me, they would be there.

We walked through fields, rather than on the roads, so that we would not be discovered. But we were; soon enough we found ourselves surrounded by German soldiers.

Although we were clearly Jews, the soldiers, perhaps relieved by the ease of their invasion, acted in a friendly manner, and even offered us a colt that had just been born to one of their mares.

There was no point in trying to travel further. It was clear that the Germans had easily occupied the entire area, and the soldiers did not seem interested in harming us. So we headed back to Govrov. We were hungry and thirsty, and on the way we drew and drank water from a muddy well — using rags and handkerchiefs to strain the water somewhat. There is a Yiddish blessing that wishes that "you not be tested by something one can get used to." It means to say that a person, if he is forced to, can get used to almost anything. Who among us ever before imagined drinking muddy water?

We arrived back in Govrov late Friday afternoon.

Any sense of security we may have felt, though, was shattered soon enough. My family and I were lying on the floor of a local Jew's house when we heard angry banging on the door and the gruff, loud words *"Raus Jude! Raus Jude!"* — "Jew, out!"

These visitors were not simple German soldiers, but member of the SS, the Schutzstaffel — the Nazi military organization that operated separately from the regular German army. SS members swore allegiance to Hitler, and they hated Jews.

The SS men chased us from the houses, prodding us with bayonets to raise our hands and join the town's other Jews — several hundred people — in the middle of the town's market area. As we walked, hands raised, the Nazis photographed us.

Some of the Germans approached the men among us who had beards and cut them off, either entirely or purposely leaving an odd angle of beard, just to humiliate the victims. One man had a beautiful, long beard. When he saw what the Germans were doing, he took a towel he had with him and tied it around his beard, in the hope that our tormentors might not see so enticing a target. But of course, they went right over to him, removed the towel and shaved off what to him and us was a physical symbol of experience, wisdom and holiness. He wept uncontrollably.

We stood there and the smell of smoke in our nostrils became more intense with each minute. It didn't take long to realize that the town's homes had been set aflame. Later we heard that a German soldier had been discovered killed nearby and that the SS men had assumed that the culprits were Jews.

Eventually the non-Jews were permitted to go out into the countryside, along with their cows and goats. We Jews were ordered into the synagogue.

My mother's sister's husband, Chaim Gelchinsky (a cousin of hers, as Gelchinsky was my mother's maiden name too), seized the opportunity to try to escape by joining the group of non-Jews. But one of them pointed him out to an SS man and said, simply, "Jew." Without a second's hesitation, the German raised his pistol and shot my uncle dead. Several other Jews were killed at that time as well.

In the synagogue, we sat terrified. Some of the people had been wounded. One elderly woman had a gaping bullet wound in her stomach. To this day I have never been able to wipe that image from my memory.

A German entered and began to remove young people, saying that they were being conscripted to work. When they came to my brother Fischel, my parents begged them to leave him with us. Fischel's hand was slightly deformed and they pointed it out to the Germans, who then left him alone.

It wasn't long, though, before my parents were wailing in regret for that ploy. It had become clear that all of us remaining in the synagogue were being confined there — the doors were locked and SS men stood outside to ensure that no one managed to escape — in order to roast us alive. The town had been set afire, and the Nazis clearly intended to let the flames reach the synagogue. Houses nearby were already wildly burning. "Why hadn't we let Fischel go?" my parents cried bitterly. "At least he could have escaped this fate!"

The scene was a blizzard of shouting and wailing and, above all, praying. Psalms and lamentations and entreaties blended together, a cacophony of wrenched hearts. Everyone realized what was in store and there was nothing, absolutely nothing, that any of us could possibly do.

Second week of October, 1939 (end of Tishrei, 5700)

Maybe it was the memory of their anguish at not having allowed the Germans to conscript Fischel that pushed my parents to let me, their 14-year old, board a train mere weeks later to a place I had never seen, at the very start of a war. They were certainly wise enough to realize that in such times, no one can know, as the Yom Kippur prayer puts it "who will live and who will die" — which path might lead to doom and which, unlikely though it might seem, might lead to freedom. Whatever their reason, though, I had made my decision and they made theirs.

The truck with Fischel on it, like my mother moments earlier, grew smaller as the train gained speed.

September 9, 1939 (25 Elul, 5699)

ELIJAH'S STRANGEST COSTUME

The smell of smoke grew even stronger, as did the cries of the hundreds of Jews packed in the synagogue awaiting a terrible death. And then a miracle occurred.

How else to explain what happened? Those in the synagogue who were standing near the doorway and windows saw a German motorcycle come to a halt in front of the building. A German officer – apparently of high rank – dismounted from the machine and began to speak with the SS men guarding our intended crematorium. The officer grew agitated and barked some orders at the other Nazis. After a few minutes, the doors to the synagogue were suddenly opened and, in disbelief at our good fortune, we all staggered out.

The officer, apparently, had heard the terrible din from within the building and had stopped to see what was happening. Presumably the SS men told him that the Jews had killed one of their men. What made the officer order them to release us we did not know and never will. Some of us suspected he was not a German at all, but Elijah the prophet, who, in Jewish tradition, often appears in disguise.

We were ordered across a nearby brook and some of the soldiers even carried elderly people who could not easily cross through the shallow water on their own. We were told to sit on the grass and to go no further. And so there we sat, all through the Sabbath, watching as the synagogue in which we had been imprisoned mere hours earlier was claimed by the flames and, along with all the Torah-scrolls and holy books of both Ruzhan and Govrov, burned to the ground. During the night that followed, some men ventured forth to bury the dead of previous days, my uncle among them. In Judaism, a body is not to be left unburied for long if there is any way of returning it to the earth.

That night was the first night of Selichos, the special entreaties for forgiveness of sins that are recited before Rosh Hashana and Yom Kippur.

It was cold, with autumn unmistakably in the air, and we, the live Jews, huddled together through the night, shivering from both the chill and the unknown.

When morning came, though, there was not a soldier to be seen. All the Nazis had left. We went back into the town. There we found a bizarre blessing amid the destruction: Several pear trees, laden with fruit, stood like sad, silent witnesses to all that had happened to the town. The fruit on the branches had been baked by the flames. We picked and ate the pears, a delicious, unexpected delicacy — a dessert unattached to any meal. But the gift was a goodbye present; nothing else was left of the town. And so we moved on.

End of September, 1939 (Tishrei, 5700)

A FESTIVAL AMID CHAOS

We came to a town, Dlugosiodlo, whose population was a mixture of Jews, Germans and Poles, and we stayed there for several weeks, through the High Holy Days of Rosh Hashana and Yom Kippur – the holiest day of the Jewish year. We held services but, expecting German soldiers to arrive in the town, feared what they might do if they found us praying. As we knew from the way they treated the men with beards back in the Govrov marketplace, most Germans saw Jews as something beyond just another conquered people. They hated us, viscerally and intensely, for who we were.

Yom Kippur is followed, five days later, by the holiday of Sukkos. We tried the best we could to make it a festive time, and even built a *sukkah*, the thatch-roofed hut from which the holiday takes its name. On the intermediary days of the holiday, an airplane flew very low over the city. Everyone ran into the houses but I was so fascinated by the sight of the machine – I had probably never seen one before – that I stood outside staring at it in wonder. Until, that is, my parents pulled me into the house where we were staying.

On the eighth and final day of that holiday, which is called Shemini Atzeres, a bus filled with many Nazi soldiers arrived in the town and once again all the Jews were chased from the homes where they had taken refuge into the town marketplace. A grossly overweight German soldier climbed on top of the bus and, in Polish, told us to "Go to your brothers in Zembrov" – a town several miles away. He made clear that anyone who defied his suggestion would be shot. We had no intention of testing his sincerity and, after gathering our few things from the houses where we had been staying, we began, once again, to walk.

Which we did the entire day and that night, through a thick forest, stopping only for prayer services, so that men — including my father — could recite the Kaddish, a special prayer recited by a mourner for eleven months after the loss of a parent. My grandfather Lazer Elya Der Melamed had died shortly before the German invasion.

It was the final day of the holiday period, Simchas Torah, an especially joyous day on the Jewish calendar. We spent it trudging through a downpour, stopping to get some bread at a town called Ostrow Mazowiecka, on the Polish side of the war border, which we then crossed, making our way to Zembrov, which was in the part of Poland under Russian control.

It was later revealed that Jews who tried to remain in Dlugosiodlo were found by the Nazis and killed on the spot. A woman who owned a grocery store was buried alive, as was the town *shochet*, or ritual slaughterer, one Reb Pinchas. Even though he had been shot before being buried, he managed to later climb out of the grave, and eventually made his way to Bialystok. An older man who remained in the town to care for his pregnant daughter was caught by the Nazis, who took off all his clothes and forced him to flee, unclothed in the cold fall weather, for their entertainment.

As for us, we finally reached the temporary border that separated the German-occupied part of Poland from the section the Russians controlled. The skies were still pouring rain, and water sloshed in the buckets into which all who were passing from one side of the border to the other were to deposit their valuables. They held a cold stew of coins, stopwatches, buckles and trinkets.

We had nothing of value, not even a watch, but my parents had some Polish currency and, even before the holidays, they had sewn it into the lining of my coat so that when things settled down — they hoped — they would have something with which to buy the necessities of life.

On Simchas Torah, Jews complete the yearly cycle of Torah-readings. We read the very last part of the Torah and then immediately begin it anew. It is a time of celebration, a day when Jews customarily dance while holding Torah scrolls. We had no Torahs anymore, but we danced all the same. It was Simchas Torah, after all, and we in fact did have something to celebrate. We had escaped the Germans.

And when we saw a short Russian soldier with a pointy hat standing under a tree to escape the rain, we started dancing again. After all, he wasn't a Nazi.

When we reached Zembrov, we found the town synagogue, where we prayed and were offered some food. It was Friday and so we remained in the town for the Sabbath — Shabbos Beraishis, when the first part of the Torah is read publicly. There were some abandoned Polish military barracks in the town and so we occupied a corner of the building; it carried the stench of blood and filth but served us as a temporary home until better arrangements could be found.

It was the next day that I announced to my parents that I was leaving to go to the Bialystok yeshiva, where I was supposed to have traveled weeks earlier.

They reacted, understandably, with shock. The war is not over, they said. They had no idea how right they were, how many years and lives it would take until peace would come to Europe. I was all of fourteen and had never even been on a train, they reminded me. I had never been farther away from home than Ostrolenka. They were right there too.

But I also knew that I had promised myself that I was going to yeshiva, and I had no intention of breaking my promise.

I convinced them. Or, more likely, they just realized that I wasn't going to be budged. And they probably wondered if, considering that they had no idea what the future held for them, I might not be better off somewhere else. If that was their reasoning, they were right once again.

Having received my father's blessing, some apples from my mother and a kiss from each, I went to the local train station. My mother accompanied me.

> ### *Second week of October, 1939 (end of Tishrei, 5700)*
>
> *Fischel's face became a speck in the distance and then the truck did the same, finally disappearing entirely.*
>
> *I would never again see Fischel, or my father or my mother.*

PART II

Exile's Hidden Blessing

October, 1939 (End of Tishrei, 5700)

SIMCHA, GET ON THE TRAIN!

On the train, two elderly Jews with long beards approached me and asked "*Yingeleh, vu forst tu?*" – "Little boy where are you going?"

"To the Bialystok Yeshiva," I replied.

"The Bialystok yeshiva?" they repeated. "The Bialystok yeshiva isn't in Bialystok anymore! It moved to Vilna!"

In fact, as I later discovered, all the Polish yeshivos had moved to Vilna.

My journey to yeshiva was not starting off smoothly.

The famed city of Vilna had been a center of Jewish life for centuries. Napoleon, it is said, called it "the Jerusalem of Lithuania." During World War I, the city, along with the rest of Lithuania, was occupied by the German Empire but in 1918 Lithuania was declared an independent country again. Vilna itself was controlled, at various times, by Lithuania, Poland, and the Soviet Union.

With the start of the Second World War, the Soviets expanded their sphere of influence over Lithuania, setting up military bases in parts of the country. Although, in October, 1939, the Red Army withdrew from Vilna, allowing Lithuania to claim sovereignty over it, the city was still very much under "Mother Russia"'s thumb. Within a year, the Soviets would annex all of Lithuania.

The Soviets, moreover, hated religion, indeed had made a religion out of their hatred for religion. But the leaders of the yeshivos hoped, despite the Soviet boot poised above all of Lithuania, that Vilna's contested status – and the Soviets' assurance to Lithuania that the city would retain its sovereignty – might provide some time and a means for them and their students to leave Europe altogether. That the thousand-year European Jewish sojourn in Eastern Europe was coming to an end was a foregone conclusion. All that remained to be seen was who would manage to escape, how and to where.

Having cast my lot with the Bialystok yeshiva – wherever it might actually happen to be – I convinced myself that all that had changed was my trip itinerary. Just as I had been headed to Bialystok, now I was headed to Vilna. I had never been to either place, so it really made no difference.

When the train arrived in Bialystok, I got off and wandered around the station looking for a train to Vilna. A long line of people stood at the ticket counter. I joined the line and began asking people where I could find the train to Vilna and how I might buy a ticket. No one seemed to know but then a man, overhearing my questions, came over to me and pointed toward a train. I told him I had no ticket. "Don't worry," he said. "Just get on the train."

So I ran, across several rail tracks, although it was dark and I could not see if any other trains were coming. I reached the place where the man had pointed and confirmed that it was the Vilna train. Vilna was clearly the place to go; people were crammed into the train, hanging from its doors. There seemed no way I could ever get on board. My confidence began to crumble and, standing there among the trains and the travelers, I began to cry. Something within me, though, insisted that, somehow, I had to get on the train. It was as if some voice were shouting at me "Simcha, get on the train!" As I stood there, the chugging machine began to pull out of the station.

The silent but insistent voice inside me ordered my feet to walk, then trot, alongside the slowly moving metal monster. My only hope was to join those packed on the steps attached to the outside of the train. I found myself grabbing the handle alongside the steps. Hoisting myself up, I found a spot for one of my feet. The train began to move faster. I hung on tightly.

When we approached full speed, people who had been hanging outside the train began to push themselves in; those in the car had somehow made room for some of them. I was a small boy and managed to get inside myself, though I could not find any space to sit down, other than the small platform between two of the train's cars. Later I learned that the train had been the very last one to make the trip from Bialostok to Vilna, and that other young men from various yeshivas would later be forced to use dangerous means to smuggle themselves across the border from Russian-controlled Poland to Lithuania.

So I was more fortunate than I knew at the time. And exhausted. There on the platform I fell asleep. When I awoke, it was the next morning and we were in Vilna.

I knew no one in the city but reassured myself that, well, I didn't know anyone in Bialystok either, so I wasn't any worse off for the change of plans. When I fully opened my eyes, I saw a young Jewish man with a small beard standing nearby. I stood up and approached him. "I'm looking for the Bialystok yeshiva," I said, "now in Vilna."

"So am I," he said, smiling.

Suddenly, I wasn't alone anymore.

We got off the train and, after wandering around the city a bit and asking directions from strangers — everyone, after all, in this new world was a stranger — we finally found the yeshiva. We were warmly welcomed by the students and faculty, and quickly settled into the rhythm of study, prayer and introspection that was the Novardhok Yeshiva.

Founded in Russia a half century earlier, Novardhok was more than a yeshiva; it was a phenomenon, a living expression of the "Mussar Movement" established in the middle of the 19th century to stress and cultivate perfection of character and purity of motive among Jews.

A story is told of how a freethinker once asked to meet with the founder of Novardhok, Rabbi Yosef Yoizel Horowitz (known as the "Der Alter" — "the Elder" — of Novardhok) and was welcomed into the revered rabbi's home. The two began to discuss the meaning of life, the concept of being commanded by G-d and the imperative of improving one's character. After some hours of deep discussion, the freethinker turned to his servant and ordered him to prepare his carriage for his journey home. The Alter abruptly ended the conversation then and there.

Puzzled at the sudden interruption of what seemed to be a productive back-and-forth, the guest asked his host if he had perhaps done something wrong. The Alter calmly explained that, for him, a conversation like the one they had been having was no mere philosophical sparring, not an intellectual exercise and certainly not a social pleasantry. It was a means of ascertaining truths, with the determined goal of acting on them. Had the freethinker seen their conversation the same way, said the Alter, he would have been transfixed, weighing the impact the concepts they had clarified must have on his life — and would have been simply unable to leave before clarifying things fully and making important decisions about his future.

By deciding instead that their "time was up" and it was time to go, said the Alter, his guest had demonstrated that the interaction had all been of just a theoretical nature, an intellectual debate. For such things, the rabbi demurred, he simply had no time. There were important things to get done.

That seriousness of purpose is what defined Novardhok. The yeshiva's particular approach involved training oneself to be unconcerned with honor or comfort. The ego was to be treated as a servant, not a master. Toward that end, the most successful Novardhok students purposefully wore tattered clothing ; and some, it is widely reported, deliberately acted in ways that would normally evoke embarrassment or discomfort. Stories of Novardhokers going to a bakery and asking for a box of nails, or putting pebbles in their shoes are legend.

Whether they are accurate or not, though, they do reflect the spiritual goal that Novardhok impressed on its students: to rise above the petty feelings, emotional or physical, that dictate most people's actions. Only service to G-d matters, and the freedom that comes from not caring about what people might be saying or what one might be feeling allows a person to focus entirely on what is most important in life: service to G-d.

The spiritual self-discipline that Novardhok stressed also strengthens a person, insulating him from the fear of shame or pain, providing, oddly enough, a powerful self-confidence — and it provides its adherents the ability to face whatever adversity may confront him later in life. For many of Novardhok's students those days, that ability would serve them well.

After the Russian Revolution, the Novardhok yeshiva left Russia — Communism abhorred religion, and had no tolerance at all for as serious and determined an expression of religious faith as Novardhok. The Alter decided to move the yeshiva to Poland. The move was fraught with peril, and many students were shot or banished to Siberia in the process, but several hundred made it across the border.

After Rabbi Horowitz's death, the main yeshiva was established in Bialystok, under the leadership of his son-in-law, Rabbi Avrohom Yoffen. From that central study-hall, teams of students were dispatched to Polish cities and towns far and wide, to evaluate whether the Jewish communities there were fertile grounds for the establishment of a Novardhok branch. More than seventy proved to be. The Bialystok "main yeshiva" was the one that had again been forced to relocate, now to Vilna; it was the one I was privileged to join.

November, 1939 (Cheshvan, 5700)

OPEN VILNA, ELUSIVE VISAS

Coordinating the affairs of the many yeshivos that had relocated to Vilna was the famous Jewish scholar and leader, Rabbi Chaim Ozer Grodzinsky. He had arranged for each of the yeshivos to find a new physical home in a local synagogue, of which there were many. Bais Yosef, the Novardhok yeshiva, had taken refuge in what was called the "Gesher Hayorok Shul", or "Green Bridge Synagogue" – named for a nearby river crossing that was painted green.

We stayed there for a while, not just studying but sleeping in the synagogue, as there was no other available housing for us. Rav Chaim Ozer tried to help all the yeshivos to the degree he could, and obtained some bread for us.

We slept on the floor without blankets; we wore our coats to keep warm. I remember thinking that usually when people say they are going to sleep, they are not really speaking precisely. When *I* went to sleep, though, I really *went* to sleep, putting my coat on as if I were actually headed somewhere. The thought brought a smile to my face.

During the week some food was brought into the synagogue for us to eat between classes. On Shabbos, though, we were assigned as guests to various local homes of Jewish families who had volunteered to help feed the yeshiva boys. At the first home to which I was sent I was surprised to be served black bread on Shabbos, rather than the customary white challah. I didn't expect to be pampered, of course; it was wartime, after all, but I was struck all the same by the simple fare. When I took my first bite, though, I was surprised again – at how wonderfully delicious it was. Trying circumstances, I discovered, can heighten the pleasure of simple things.

As it happened, we didn't remain in Vilna very long. At the end of 1939, Rav Chaim Ozer and the other rabbinical leaders of the community had decided that the best way to preserve the safety and integrity of the yeshivas was to have each of them relocate to a different Lithuanian town.

Our yeshiva was assigned to Birzh (probably the town identified on maps today as Birzai) and the town provided a blissfully peaceful environment for us. The Jewish townsfolk supported the physical needs of the students, and our study sessions were well organized and functioned smoothly. We even had rooms in which to sleep and a kitchen of our own. It was, all in all, very much like what I had always imagined normal yeshiva life to be.

Although I was a younger student, I sometimes was honored to be the reader of the weekly Torah portion, just as my older brother Fischel, an excellent Torah reader, had done back in Ruzhan. But I was still not very experienced at Torah-reading and remember a mistake I made on the Monday or Thursday before the Shabbos when we read the Torah portion of Pinchas. (On those days of the week, the first part of the weekly portion is read in shul.) I may have read the portion well but I paused when I spied a letter in the Torah that seemed to have not been written properly, and stopped reading. As it happened, though – and as I was quickly informed – the letter, the *vov* of the word "*sholom*," "peace" – is supposed to be written in an unusual way, with a break between the letter's top half and bottom.

Pinchas, the subject of that portion, is traditionally associated with Eliyohu, or Elijah the prophet, who according to Jewish tradition will one day herald the coming of Moshiach, or the Messiah. Then, the tradition has it, the *vov* of *sholom* will be restored to its full form. It was 1940, though, and neither the Messiah nor peace had yet arrived.

We remained in Birzh until the spring of 1941. During our months there, I heard from my parents, to whom I had written when the yeshiva was still in Vilna, to let them know where I was and that I was fine. Several cards from them postmarked Zembrov somehow made their way to Birzh. Although they contained little hard information, the short letters filled me with hope for my parents' wellbeing. The last card I received from them, though, was from a different town. I realized that the new postmark could only mean one thing: the German advance had continued and my parents were once again on the run.

There was, of course, no way I could have predicted either their future or mine. Especially when, during our sojourn in Birzh, the Soviets officially annexed all of Lithuania, putting an end to any independence the country had (or would have, until 1990).

All the yeshiva boys and rabbis realized that the time had come to leave —
Lithuania for certain, Europe if possible. Visas were sought for anyplace anywhere
in the world — China, Japan, Madagascar, South America. If a consulate indi-
cated its willingness to provide a visa, the document would be eagerly snatched
up. Needless to say, such tickets out of the roiling European cauldron were not
easily found.

A LONGER TRAIN RIDE, EASTWARD

In 1941, the Soviets – probably realizing that a German invasion of their territories was likely – decreed that all refugees had to take on Soviet citizenship. Doing so, of course, meant servitude to the Soviet Union and, for those of able body, service – and likely death – on the future Soviet-German battlefield. Refusing the offer, however, meant that one was a foreign national during wartime, and a presumed enemy of the state. It was a status that carried its own considerable risks.

The run for visas, understandably, became even more urgent. Our yeshiva received only two, one for the head of the yeshiva, Rabbi Avrohom Yoffen; the other for one of his students and future son-in-law, Chaim Boruch Faskowitz. Rabbi Yoffen's other son-in-law, Rabbi Yehudah Leib Nekritz, would take Rabbi Yoffen's place as the head of the yeshiva.

That summer, the Soviets posted a list of those who had refused their offer of citizenship, summoning them to turn themselves in to the authorities. My fellow yeshiva students and I were on the list, of course, and so was Rabbi Nekritz.

When, on the first day of the holiday of Shavuos, the Soviet police came to the yeshiva to round up the students, all of us panicked at the thought of what awaited us at Soviet hands. I and a friend of mine, Pinchas Menachem Malach, tried to hide. We ran up to the upper story of the building and into a small room that we imagined – "hoped" would be a better word – the searchers would overlook. We barricaded ourselves inside, putting benches and chairs up against the door.

The authorities, as one can imagine, were not deterred by our efforts. When they had trouble opening the door they probably realized that it was worth breaking down, which they then commenced to do. Once they had pushed the furniture out of their way, it wasn't hard for them to grab us. They took us to a railroad yard, where a long line of train cars awaited us, along with all the other Jewish refugees who had refused to accept Soviet citizenship.

This train was not a "luxurious" one like the one I had pulled myself onto back in Bialystok. These were cattle cars, intended now for two-legged livestock. And this time the voice telling me to board wasn't in my head; it was a soldier's. I had no choice. But this train, too, like the ones I boarded back in Zembrov and Bialystok, was destined to save my life. Whether through a message only I could hear or a Russian soldier, G-d was guiding me.

We were loaded aboard what we all understood would be a long ride to Siberia, the Soviet Union's famed and faithful dumping ground for human beings it didn't like.

Entire families were added to our car, which was equipped with only long shelves along the walls to serve as beds, and a hole in the middle of the floor, for use as a toilet. We rigged a sheet from the ceiling of the car to curtain off the hole from its surroundings and preserve at least some measure of human dignity in our very inhuman prison on wheels. One day, when we would come to know what conditions were like in other trains transporting other Jews — boxcars packed beyond capacity and headed for death camps — we would realize that our own accommodations at the time were a four-star hotel by comparison. But they were bad enough. The train remained stationary for several days.

Rabbi Nekritz was put on the train as well, but his wife — the daughter of the yeshiva's dean Rabbi Yoffen, and a granddaughter of the famed "Alter" of Novardhok, and their two children, were not. For some reason, they had not been placed on the Soviet list of deportees. Mrs. Nekritz begged the guards to allow her and the children to join their husband and father but they refused. After many tears and much pleading, however, they finally relented and granted the family the privilege of being part of our special "Orient Express."

The locals thought Mrs. Nekritz had lost her mind. Just because her husband was being sent to Siberia was no reason to cast her own fate, and those of their two small daughters, to the same ill wind. But her decision, in the end, saved her and their lives.

When the soldiers guarding the trains walked out of sight of our car, some of the boys from the yeshiva whose names for some reason had not been on the list brought us Hebrew holy books, food, and some articles of clothing. They knew where we were headed and that we would need things to keep both our souls and our bodies nourished and warm.

They pitied us greatly, shedding tears and mourning our lot, banishment to Siberia. As it turned out, though, with G-d's help we would survive. What happened to the "fortunate" ones who remained behind, however, is unknown. One thing is certain: later that year, 1941, the Nazis, may their names be blotted from human memory, would occupy the Baltic states, including Lithuania.

And so, although they didn't know or intend it, the Russians had preserved us. The war, which until then had been limited to Poland, Russia and Germany, was entering its second stage, when it would involve all the major world powers. A regional conflict had metastasized into a World War.

It is usually referred to as the "Jager Report," after its author, SS-Standartenfuhrer Karl Jager, whose name means "hunter" in German. His hunting ground was Lithuania; his prey, Jews.

The report is dated December 1, 1941 and marked "Secret Reich Business." Its content is a "complete list of executions carried out in the EK [Einsatzkommando] 3 area" until that date. It begins with an entry for July 2, 1941, when, in Vilna, "on my instructions and order," Lithuanian partisans killed 416 Jews and 47 Jewesses. The document, as throughout, starkly tallies the total for the reader's convenience: "463."

The Jager Report then notes a "raiding squad" under the command of the improbably named SS-Obersturmfuhrer Hamann that resulted in the killing — with the "cooperation" of "Lithuanian partisans," of 3384 men and women, mostly Jews, in a number of towns, carefully listed along with the dates of their invasions.

7.7.41 Mariampole Jews 32, 26 Jewesses . . .
21.7.41 Panevezys 59 Jews, 11 Jewesses. . .
23.7.41 Kedainiai 83 Jews, 12 Jewesses. . .

Good accountant's report that it is, the document's second sheet begins with the words "Total carried over: 3,384." It then proceeds to list dozens more Lithuanian towns — Darsuniskis,

Carliava, Petrasiunai, Babtei, Wenziogal. . . — names lost to history, each followed by the number of "Jews," "Jewesses," "Jewish children" and others who were systematically murdered there by their hunters.

The "Total carried forward" to the next page is: "16,152."

Among the victims listed are 43 in Uzusalis, killed on September 11 and 12, 1941 as a "reprisal against inhabitants who fed Russian partisans"; 1608 Jews in Kauen, including "581 Jewish children (sick and suspected epidemic cases)"; another 9200 Jewish men, women and children in that same city on October 29, as a "mopping up [of the] ghetto of superfluous Jews"; yet another 2934 there who were "resettlers from Berlin, Munich and Frankfurt Am Main." There is the "1 Reichs German who converted to the Jewish faith and attended rabbinical school"; and the many thousands who were murdered over a number of days in Vilna;

By sheet 4, the "Total carried over" is 47,814.

At the end of sheet 6 comes the grand total: 137,346.

And then the report's closing sentences:

"Today I can confirm that our objective, to solve the Jewish problem for Lithuania, has been achieved by EK 3. In Lithuania

there are no more Jews, apart from Jewish workers and their families.

"The distance from the assembly point to the graves was on average 4 to 5 Km.

"I consider the Jewish action more or less terminated as far as Einsatzkommando 3 is concerned. Those working Jews and Jewesses still available are needed urgently and I can envisage that after the winter this workforce will be required even more urgently. I am of the view that the sterilization program of the male worker Jews should be started immediately so that reproduction is prevented. If despite steriliza-tion a Jewess becomes pregnant she will be liquidated."

The order is signed: Jager, SS-Standartenfuhrer

PART III

A Forbidding Refuge

June-July 1941 (Sivan-Tamuz, 5701)

ADJUSTING TO NEW ACCOMMODATIONS

Our train began to move, and gained speed as it headed eastward. The journey took weeks. Although the car was crowded, we would make our way to a corner when it was time to pray, and did so with a *minyan*, the prayer-quorum of ten men. We would also study with Rabbi Nekritz when we could. Much of the time we lay on the makeshift bunks that lined the walls of the train, and pondered our lives, our responsibilities as Jews, and what trials the future held for us.

Occasionally, the train would stop at some station, and we would be given a piece of bread and some hot water – which was all that prevented us from arriving in Siberia as mere bodies to be buried. And as we headed east, we saw other trains, many of them, on parallel tracks, heading in the opposite direction; they pulled platforms on which there were tanks and other military equipment. We understood that the Russian armaments were being transported for use at the front against the Germans, who were advancing into the part of Poland then occupied by Russia.

Finally, we arrived in Novosibirsk, the large city at the onset of Siberia, the easternmost end of the rail line.

The guards took us off the train there, and put us on a barge, since the only way deeper into Siberia was by river. That water journey also seemed to take weeks, although time had become a slippery thing. Our particular group's destination was a town called Nizhna Machavaya – Lower Machavaya. There we were to stay, ten young men – boys would better have described most of us – and their teacher, Rabbi Nekritz; his wife and their two daughters; and several other Jewish families who happened to have been loaded onto our train car back in Birzh.

When we reached Nizhna Machavaya, at the end of July, 1941 (Tamuz, 5701) and disembarked, the guards told us "This is where you will be living." Then they added: "And you will have to work hard to do any eating."

It was a message that had clearly been delivered to many who had arrived there before us.

The vast western part of Siberia, where we found ourselves, is taiga, a dense forest of spruce, cedar, pine and fir trees. The forest floor is covered with moss and, of course, in winter — a long season, lasting from September to May — snow.

A few weeks into the cold season there would be several feet of it, and it would remain until the late spring thaw. During the warm season, birds seen nowhere else on earth for some unfathomable reason make the Siberian taiga their home, or at least a way station from one point to another; and a host of insects, beautiful butterflies as well as stinging gnats and mosquitoes, had also preceded us to Siberia. Squirrels, voles and other rodents skittered around and the forest harbored foxes, deer and brown bears — the latter often a concern of ours when we were at work in the wilderness.

The "*natchalnik*," or "boss" — the government functionary for the village — assigned all the newcomers to their lodgings. He reported to the NKVD, the feared Soviet secret service, whose regional office was based in Parbig, a city several miles to the west. We nicknamed the boss "Bez Noza" — "missing a nose" — as it well described his unfortunate but hard to ignore physical appearance. Over the course of our about two years in Siberia, a NKVD officer from Parbig would regularly show up in Nizhna Machavaya to lecture us about the wonders of Communism, the importance of hard work for the state, how the war was proceeding and other such pressing matters.

A friend, Shlomo Figa (who was also called Shlomo Makover, after his home town), and I were assigned to a family that had lived in Nizhna Machavaya for years. The family members — and now we along with them — lived in a one room hut. The man of the house, a Russian citizen, was absent, having been drafted into the army. His wife slept on a bunk-bed in one corner of the house; we in another, on the floor; and the woman's elderly mother-in-law on a wall cot above the oven. Considering the climate most of the year, it was without question the best bed in the house.

Our hosts had certainly not asked for nonpaying tenants but, like most Russians those days, simply accepted their government's demands as a matter of course. They did not treat us badly in any way, although they made sure we realized how good we had it.

As did all the locals. "When we were brought here years ago," they told us new arrivals, "there was nothing."

"The authorities gave us axes and shovels and saws," they recounted, "and left us to clear the taiga for fields and build our own houses."

"You are the lucky ones," they would say, and, that fact established, we were put to work, overseen by the Russian *natchalnik*. Whatever they ordered us to do, we did. There were trees to fell, there was wood to chop, grain to harvest and grind. There were potatoes and onions to dig up, and wagons to load. There was never any lack of work.

Sometimes, several of us were fortunate to be assigned to work together. Harvesting grain and chopping down trees, for instance, were done in teams. When we found ourselves working in pairs or as a group, we would take the opportunity to review pages of Talmud or recite Tehillim together.

We arrived in late summer, and during those hot months, we would supplement the meager bread ration we received by picking what fruit, berries or wild vegetation – like small onions – we could find. Some of us were able to eat a bit of the raw grain we harvested or the flour we ground. But there were quotas that had to be filled in order for us to receive our bread rations, so helping ourselves to even that unappetizing nourishment was not a regular option.

During the Siberian summer the insects were a constant plague. There were times when one or another of us would return from working in the forest and be almost unrecognizable because his face was swollen with insect bites. We thought that the summer must be the most trying season in Siberia. Until winter arrived, of course, which happened well before the High Holy Days, a time of year we had always experienced as a temperate fall season. Then we quickly realized that the worst was yet to come.

When winter and its sub-zero temperatures arrived – 40 degrees below zero was not unusual – our host families on occasion allowed us to use their oven for cooking. We were very happy when they did, since the only food besides the meager portion of bread we received was our special delicacy: frozen potatoes.

We would search for potatoes that had escaped the harvest in the warmer season, survivors left on the now-frozen soil. When they thawed out, we would cut the now rubbery tubers into strips which we placed on the top of the metal stove. Yield: a foodlike substance that might be described as a very distant and very poor relative of what we would one day know as french fries. To us, of course, the potato strips were mouth-watering.

The frigid cold, meager food and hard labor were simply the cost of staying alive. And we worked hard. A major part of the workload was cutting down large trees in the forest — three of us holding hands would just manage to encompass a typical tree's circumference. We were told that the wood was to be used to make the shafts of rifles to be used by the Soviet army on the war front.

The major challenge for us came with the arrival of the Sabbath. The locals insisted that we work every day of the week, but we refused on Shabbos. They threatened to shoot us, singling out Rabbi Nekritz, knowing that if they broke him, we would likely follow his example. But he stood firm. He told them calmly in fluent Russian (although he had Polish papers, he was Russian-born and raised) that he would be willing to do things that might meet the authorities' definition of work but which didn't violate Jewish religious law. Chopping down trees, though, or any sort of planting or harvesting, he said just as calmly, was forbidden to us Jews on Shabbos.

When a Jew's life is in danger, he is permitted to do even forbidden labor on the Sabbath. And some members of our group may in fact have been forced on occasion to do actual work that violated the Shabbos laws. All the same, Rabbi Nekritz must have assessed that he, at least, as the spiritual leader of the group, could safely refuse orders. At one point, threatened by our guards for such a refusal, he opened his shirt and quietly challenged them to shoot him. They backed down.

So avoiding work that would violate Shabbos became a weekly endeavor for us. We would sometimes pretend we were sick on Shabbos, although the charade was clearly transparent to the townsfolk, who not only knew we were faking but knew that we knew that they knew. I often wondered what they really thought about the crazy Jews who were willing to work hard six out of seven days but were so obstinate about that seventh.

Whatever they thought, though, sometimes they accepted the ploy, and sometimes they did not. When they didn't want to accept excuses, they would force us into the fields, where we would just stay and study or recite Tehillim.

They sometimes withheld some food from us for that violation of their rules, but at some point they stopped threatening us. We may have been crazy to them, but we earned our keep — and our Saturday work just wasn't worth the trouble to them.

I was personally very fortunate. Maybe because I was the youngest — all of sixteen at the time — in the winter I landed the steady job of field-watchman, which didn't require me to violate Shabbos. The fields of the *kolkhoz*, or collective farm, were a good distance away from the village, and after the grain had been harvested, it stood in piles awaiting transport. I simply spent the day far from the village, out in the fields, charged with chasing away any animal or man who might approach the harvested crops. I have no idea what I, a small-boned, half-starved teenager, would have even done had such a threat actually materialized but, thank G-d, it never did.

During my work time, I studied what I could from the holy books that we had, and recited many, many chapters of Tehillim.

April, 2008 (Nisan, 5768)

"Gita, in his interview my father refers to the minus-40 degree weather in the Siberian winter. I guess that's Celsius. Water's freezing point in Fahrenheit is 32 degrees, right?"

"That's right."

"So what would forty below Celsius be in Fahrenheit degrees?"

"I'm not sure. But I can look it up here."

"Could you? Thanks much. I imagine it's about zero. That's about when I feel my ears and fingers go numb at the bus stop after a few minutes. And they worked in such cold every day, the entire day! It's really hard to imagine."

"Here it is. Wait a minute. . . . No, that can't be. But it is. That's what it says. It's exactly the same: minus forty."

"The same? How can that be?"

"That's where both scales converge. Minus forty Celsius is minus forty Fahrenheit."

THE KINDNESS OF G-D, AND OF A FRIEND

That first winter was the hardest, as we did not have the proper clothing for the severe climate. The locals had boots made of pressed wool. We sufficed with layers of rags and such, in which we wrapped our hands and feet.

Even on relatively moderate winter days — when it was only freezing and not frigid — the temperature would often drop well below zero at night, though I had a small stove nearby that warmed me somewhat when I was on guard duty. The head of the *kolkhoz* would make surprise checks on me to see if I had fallen asleep, and I would recite Tehillim to stay awake.

One night, something wasn't right. I couldn't shake the chills, even huddled near the oven. Feeling very dizzy too, I suspected I had a fever. I managed to hitch my horse and sled together and set off for the *kolkhoz*. On the way, though, I lost consciousness and fell from the sled into the deep snow at the side of the road. The horse continued on without me. I tried to shout out to the animal to stop. But it just trudged on. I don't know if my attempts at shouting even yielded any sound.

I lay there in the snow crying and reciting Tehillim from memory for I knew that remaining where I was, or trying to walk to the *kolkhoz*, would mean certain death from exposure. "I will lift my eyes to the mountains," King David declared in Psalm 121, and I declared the same from my Siberian snowbank, which I considered might become my grave. "Whence will my salvation come?"

"My salvation," the Psalm continues – and so did I – "is from the L-rd, the One Who made heaven and earth."

The words somehow energized me and I managed to stand up. With what little strength I had left, I began to run after the horse and sled.

Suddenly, and I don't know why, the horse stopped in its tracks. I felt a surge of spirit and, running even faster, I reached the sled and hoisted myself onto it. Collapsed on my back, I looked up at the clear, stunningly star-filled night sky and prayed with all my diminishing might for G-d to let me reach the safety of the *kolkhoz*.

He answered me favorably. The horse, perhaps remembering the way from his many journeys back and forth to the fields, perhaps heeding a hidden Rider, eventually reached the *kolkhoz*. I was shaking uncontrollably from my fever; no number of blankets could warm me. At some point I blacked out again, and the next day, still in a daze, I was transported to Parbig, 14 kilometers away, the closest town large enough to have a hospital.

My first few days there were a blur, but at some point my fever broke and I began to feel a little better. Then, one day, as I lay in my bed, I was shocked to see one of my yeshiva comrades, Herschel Nudel (whom we called Herschel Tishivitzer, after his town), standing there before me like an apparition, half frozen, his feet wrapped in the layers of rags that served as our boots, staring back, equally wide-eyed, at me. I couldn't believe my eyes – Herschel had actually walked the frigid miles from the *kolkhoz* !

"Herschel," I cried out, "what are you doing here?"

I will never forget his answer, which came after a moment or two during which he sought his tongue.

"Yesterday," he stammered, "a townswoman from Parbig came and told us 'Simcha *umar*,' – 'Simcha has died.' And so I volunteered to come and bury you."

It took me a minute to digest his words.

Had the rumor been true, I have thought many times since, there was nothing he could have done to reverse things. Yet he had made the long, perilous journey without delay – just to see to my funeral! The word for such friendship, such dedication, hasn't been invented.

Apparently I had experienced a medical crisis one night, while unconscious. The doctors or nurses must have told a woman visiting from our village that I was not going to make it.

Thankfully, doctors and nurses can be wrong.

Late 1960s (Late 5720s)

"Doctor, is something the matter?"

"Not really. At least not now, there isn't. Your examination and tests are all fine, Rabbi Shafran. You get a clean bill of health."

"Thank G-d. But what do you mean 'at least not now'?"

"Well, you seem to have once contracted tuberculosis."

"I did?"

"Yes, you tested positive and there are telltale signs in the x-rays of your lungs. The infection is contained and dormant. But it seems you had the disease at some point."

"Really?"

"Do you remember ever having had a bad cough, high fever and dizziness, followed by a long period of extreme weakness?"

"Ah, yes. I have an idea of when I might have had those symptoms."

A COVENANT POSTPONED

That same first winter, our group was witness to a remarkable thing. Back in Lithuania, on the cattle car set to take us east, placed with us young men, Rabbi and Rebbetzin Nekritz, and several families was the wife of a rabbi whose name was Betzalel Orlanski. As the Russians prepared to send all of us who had refused Soviet citizenship to Siberia, Mrs. Orlanski found herself in our cattle car, without any idea where her husband had been taken. The couple had been childless for ten years – and Mrs. Orlanski was expecting.

Her husband, as it turned out, had been sent east too, but not as far east as our group. For some reason, though, he was released from his camp that first year of our exile. Somehow or other – this too was astonishing – he managed to find out where his wife and the rest of us had been sent. And so he set out for Nizhna Machavaya.

In the winter, the only way to reach the town was to sled along the river's frozen water. Rabbi Orlanski managed to hire a local resident with a horse and sled and set out onto the river ice toward our *kolkhoz*.

He arrived soon thereafter and was reunited with his wife, miraculously, shortly before she bore him their first child, a son. The couple, needless to say, was overjoyed, despite the deprivations of the time and place. So thankful was Rabbi Orlanski for his good fortune that he was anxious to perform his son's circumcision himself, eight days after the birth, as the Torah prescribes.

Rabbi Nekritz, though, intervened, reminding the new father that he had never before performed such surgery and therefore had no right to undertake it and run the risk of injuring his child. Others among the older members of our group made clear that they agreed, and Rabbi Orlanski was persuaded to post-pone the circumcision for a more favorable time and more professional hand.

Although that time came only years later, when the little boy, Leib, was almost four, he wanted to undergo the procedure — even though it would be done without anesthetic. He understood that being circumcised would admit him into the covenant of our forefather Abraham and make him a full member of the Jewish people.

CELEBRATING IN SIBERIA

Siberia wasn't Vilna or Birzh, that was certain; we weren't in yeshiva anymore. But we created anew what we could of the yeshiva where we were. Rabbi Nekritz was our mentor and dean, and he provided us a shining example of what it means to accept one's lot with happiness, strength and determination to serve G-d.

We had some holy books, those we had taken with us as we boarded the cattle cars in Birzh, or that had been given us by friends there who had been "spared" the journey to Siberia that saved our lives. We studied from the books whenever we could, even though any expression of religious devotion was strictly forbidden by the government, and the prohibition was taken most seriously by the local authorities.

When a few of us found ourselves together, we studied as a group. A chessboard was our defense against being discovered. Its pieces arranged in mid-game, the board would suddenly become the focus of our deep attention when we heard anyone at the door. We would lean forward over the books on our laps and intensely ponder a phantom next move.

Life in Siberia didn't present only hardships and dangers, though. It also had its opportunities. Our Jewish convictions, and Rabbi Nekritz's words and actions, made us keenly aware of the fact that wherever we were and however hard it might be, there was good to be done, service to G-d. We held Shabbos prayer services as a group – when Bez Noza wasn't around – and sang the songs that grace Jewish Sabbath tables around the world. The tunes of the Modzitzer Chassidim were favorites.

We did whatever we could, too, to observe the Jewish holidays.

Sukkos, the holiday of "tents," was our first challenge. We were afraid to ask our farmer-hosts for permission to build a *sukkah*, or temporary hut, in which, at very least, meals should be eaten over the course of the seven-day holiday. If we were betrayed to the authorities for erecting an unauthorized structure – for religious purposes yet! – we could only imagine what the repercussions might be.

One of the farmers, though, we knew to be cut of a different cloth from the others. A courteous and civilized man, he had gained our trust. And he hated the authorities, having been exiled to Siberia in the first place for anti-Soviet activities. We approached him to see if he might allow us to use an unroofed storage shed of his for the holiday. It was only a few feet tall, but tall enough to satisfy the laws that define a *sukkah*. All we would have to do was roof it with some branches and it would be perfectly kosher.

"That's all I need," he replied sarcastically, shaking his head half in a negative response and half in disbelief at the request. "If the *natchalnik* were to discover you, I'd be charged in an instant with allowing an unauthorized *sabranias*, or "assembly."

"And for *popez yet!* " he added, using the Russian word for "popes" with which the non-Jewish residents of the *kolkhoz* described us Jews (intending, no doubt, "rabbis").

It wasn't an unreasonable objection, of course. But we persisted, and assured him that we would use the shed-turned-*sukkah* only for a few minutes at a time – not the ideal fulfillment of the mitzvah of "Seven days shall you dwell in Sukkos," but a *mitzvah* all the same. Maybe it was his civil disposition, maybe our relentlessness, or maybe the sheer subversiveness of the idea appealed to him. But whatever the reason or reasons, he relented, and, laying branches over the shed's walls and hanging a piece of cloth from its opening, we transformed it from a mundane structure into a holy one.

When that first Sukkos arrived, the weather was particularly bad, with strong winds and, of course, frigid cold. Still, late that first night of the holiday, we each stole away from our assigned homes with a piece of bread and made our way to our *sukkah*. There we recited Kiddush, the sanctification prayer over wine or bread made on Jewish Sabbaths and holidays. There is a blessing, too, on the *mitzvah* of *sukkah*, but we didn't recite it. A blessing, which includes G-d's name, may only be recited when there is a clear obligation. The howling wind and cold made us uncertain about whether we were obligated in the mitzvah, which is only incumbent when there is a certain degree of comfort in the *sukkah*-dwelling.

But we did recite the "Shehecheyanu" blessing, as it refers to the holiday itself and not the *mitzvah* of *sukkah*. It goes: "Blessed are You... for having kept us alive, and preserved us and allowed us to reach this time." We made the blessing with all our hearts.

On Chanuka, we made menorahs from potatoes and candles. That was not very difficult. A festive meal on Purim, unfortunately, wasn't an option for us. But as the Siberian spring – the waning of winter would better describe it – approached, we had to plan for a bigger challenge: Pesach.

Months earlier, when we had arrived in Siberia, Passover, or Pesach, was already on our minds. We knew that *matzos* for the holiday – the Torah enjoins Jews to eat at least an olive's volume, preferably two, of specially prepared unleavened bread each of the holiday's first two nights – would have to be baked somehow. And the *matzos* had to be made from wheat that had not come in contact with water after being harvested.

And so, some of the group, as they worked in the fields, squirreled away a few kernels of wheat, carefully placing them in their pockets. This was, of course, entirely against the rules, and very dangerous. The Communist credo, though, was "from each according to his ability, to each according to his needs" and so we were really only being good Marxists. Our spiritual needs, after all, included *matzoh* that was kosher for Pesach.

Back at our lodging places, the kernels were put in a special bag, which we carefully hid where no one but we could find it.

Toward the end of the winter, we ground the kernels into flour with a small hand grinder intended for coffee beans. The flour was coarse and dark but it spiritually shone all the same, reflecting the determination and dedication to G-d and His commandments that had produced it.

As the holiday approached, though, we had to face the next obstacles between us and the *mitzvah*, or commandment, of eating *matzoh* on Pesach. Jewish tradition mandates that the dough to be baked into *matzos* be riddled with perforations, to help ensure that it not rise at all during the baking process. A special tool, essentially a sort of rolling pin with cleats, is traditionally used for that purpose; obviously, we had no such implement. And, even more important, we would need an oven, one that had been made kosher for *matzoh*-baking, which required that it be fired up to a very high heat beforehand.

There was one hut in the area that was occupied solely by a Jewish family, the Beckers, who had come from Kovno. We approached the family members and proposed that we would come to their house in the middle of the night, when all the town's residents were asleep, and fire up their oven on full blast for two hours, to make it kosher. Then we would bake matzos for ourselves and them. They agreed.

And that is just what we did. We improvised a perforation tool by whittling a piece of wood so that it could be fitted with the gear-wheels from a clock, and the gear spokes thus enlisted in our *mitzvah*, produced the tiny holes in the matzos we baked. Needless to say, the flatbreads were small and very well done, but when Pesach came, we all gathered at the hut and all of us – the Nekritzes, we yeshiva boys and the Beckers – were able to fulfill the Torah's commandment to eat unleavened bread on the night of the holiday, in remembrance of our ancestors' release from the outsized prison that was ancient Egypt. Understandably, it was a *mitzvah* that resonated strongly for us.

The rabbinical requirement to drink four cups of wine could not so easily be addressed; there was no wine and there were no grapes to be found in Siberia. But, to at least undertake some semblance of that mitzvah, we managed to obtain milk – an expensive delicacy in its own right – and used it instead. It certainly tasted of the finest wine to us.

We also had eggs, traditionally eaten at the Pesach Seder, which we had obtained by bartering some of our possessions. Some of them were frozen, but that was nothing that a bit of roasting couldn't cure.

6 Kislev, 5702 (November 26, 1941)

ENTRY IN RABBI NEKRITZ'S PERSONAL NOTEBOOK

Winter of 5702 (Wednesday of parshas Vayetzei)

I conducted a "Goral HaGra" [a means of obtaining a "siman" — or "sign" about the future — by opening a Tanach, or Jewish Bible, to a random verse] about our situation. The following verses were what appeared:

"Hungry as well as thirsty, their soul fainted within them. Then they cried out to G-d in their distress, He would rescue them from their straits. And He led them upon a straight path, to go to an inhabited city. Let them acknowledge to G-d His kindness, and to the children of men His wonders. For He sated the yearning soul with good."
(Psalms, 107:5-9)

Through prayer to G-d, things will change for the better. There will no longer be "hungry as well as thirsty" and none of the emotional pain of "their soul fainted within them."

G-D, AND THE G-DLY, IN THE WORLD

When it was possible, Rabbi Nekritz would gather us and share words of encouragement and motivation, just as he did when we were back in Birzh. The Novardhok approach to life is to aim to become a "complete person," someone whose belief in G-d is total and whose personal characteristics and spiritual natures are honed and refined. This requires constant evaluation and re-evaluation of one's life and moral development. Rabbi Nekritz sought to instill in us the importance of such things.

Part of the process of becoming "complete" is deep introspection. Such self-examination was not neglected during our Siberian sojourn either. We would find opportunities to spend a few minutes in self-imposed isolation, in a far corner of a field, or among the trees of the forest, to think about who we were, who we should be, and how best to make the journey from one to the other.

One of the locals, it has been recounted, once asked Rabbi Nekritz why he thought that he, a respected rabbi and teacher of Torah, had been reduced to the life of manual labor and exiled to the wastelands of Siberia.

His response was: "So you and your friends would see that there is a G-d in the world."

Novardhoker that he was, he then added, perhaps to the questioner, perhaps to himself, probably to both: "and so that we, too, would see that there is a G-d in the world."

For any of us who knew him, the conversation is easily imagined.

We prayed at the proper times during the week, too, whenever we could, and tried to do so as a group. When we had time between work assignments, we would gather in a secluded part of the field and immerse ourselves in prayer. We would recite Tehillim, too, especially those in which King David describes the dangers and adversaries he faced during his life, and how G-d protected him. King David's words left our lips as if they had been formed in our own hearts. I often repeated the aching yet confident words of Tehillim 121, the one I called out from the snow the night I took ill, as my horse and wagon had gone on without me. "In the day, the sun will not smite you, nor the moon by night… G-d will guard over your going and your coming, for now and forever."

Mrs., or "Rebbetzin," Nekritz, too, even as she struggled to care for her two young daughters in so hostile an environment, constantly prayed. She would recite Tehillim and beseech the Creator to allow her children to know something other than the darkness and ice and their father coming "home" at the end of each winter day's forest work with icicles hanging from his beard and moustache.

Rabbi Nekritz was a paragon of calm. Whether studying with us or offering us words of encouragement, whether working in the fields, whether being taken to or brought from the interrogations to which the NKVD, or Soviet Secret Service, regularly subjected him, he was always at ease, his face a beacon of serenity and happiness.

Reb Herschel Nudel, the friend who had come to my hospital bed thinking I was no longer among the living, remembers Rabbi Nekritz returning from a short break in wood-chopping, during which he had gone off to a remote area of the forest. He slowly removed the layers of rags that served as his gloves, washed his hands carefully with snow and recited the "Asher Yatzar" blessing (made after tending to one's personal needs) slowly and deliberately, with a peaceful countenance, even though removing one's hand-coverings for even a few minutes in the well-below-zero temperature was courting frostbite.

Avi was a shy 5-year old and didn't particularly appreciate guests or commotion. When someone he didn't know would visit his home in the lower Park Heights neighborhood of Baltimore, he would generally run off and hide in some corner of the house.

One guest, though, intrigued the boy. Avi didn't really know who he was, the man with the black hat, white beard and so. . . peaceful a smile. But he knew the mystery rabbi had something

to do with his father, and watched as his parents warmly welcomed the guest as he entered the front door into the small house's living room.

For his part, Avi quickly ran to the far end of the adjacent dining room, where he sat under the table and, from a safe distance, carefully studied the bright, cheery eyes above the visitor's ruddy cheeks, and the beatific smile nestled within his snow-white beard.

To this day, five decades later, Avi recalls what he did, and recalls just as clearly, too, not knowing why. Something welled up inside him and the child found himself bounding across the room — it was only a few yards, but many, many little-boy steps — and hurling himself onto the visitor's lap. Rabbi Yehudah Leib Nekritz and his hosts were as surprised as was Avi at himself. Rabbi Nekritz's smile, though, only broadened, as he gave his new friend a kiss.

In Siberia, we learned what prayer really means. We had no idea how long our exile would last, or indeed if it would ever end. We never knew if we would survive the week, the month, the year. Or, we shuddered to think, the years.

We were specks in a vast frozen taiga, thousands of miles from our homes. No, even farther, because our homes, we knew, weren't there anymore. They might just as well be on one of the countless, nameless stars that sparkled serenely in the clear Siberian night sky. History had spoken; things could not unhappen. And so we prayed, fervently, sincerely, with every muscle in our aching hearts — for the welfare of those we had left behind, and for ourselves.

Our prayer and our study — even out in the fields and forests, we reviewed passages we knew by heart — were priceless in themselves, but they also infused us with an emotional strength that banished hopelessness from our hearts. When we allowed our Jewish souls full expression, we felt that Siberia, somehow, would not prove to be our end, that there would be a future for us. Rabbi Nekritz would often tell us – looking back now, prophetically – that one day, with G-d's help, we would be in a better place, and that, in fact, we would look upon our Siberian sojourn as a precious time of spiritual growth.

And so, whatever our future would turn out to be, a time of growth was indeed what we tried to make our present. In the Novardhoker tradition of focus on refining one's character, Rabbi Nekritz would deliver regular lectures on *mussar*, or religio/ethical, topics. And we eagerly absorbed his insights, his exhortations and his example.

From a Lecture delivered by Rabbi Nekritz, Winter, 5704/1943

"Among the great Sages of the Talmud were men who had professions. Rav Yitzchak Nafcha was a nafcha, a blacksmith, a lowly job. When we picture a blacksmith, we imagine someone with grossly muscular arms and an unrefined soul. Yet Rav Yitzchak Nafcha was one of the illustrious Jewish scholars of all time, and possessed the same holiness and refinement of any of the Sages. The same sublime spiritual nature of a sage whose fortune was to exclusively study Torah all the days of his life infused those who did even the most lowly work. Their lot in life did not affect their spiritual growth in any way.

"Yes, our situation here is very different from what it was in yeshiva. But we can strengthen ourselves so that our surroundings and our labors do not have an effect on our souls. One can be a woodchopper and simultaneously develop an exalted, refined soul, as exalted and refined as that of anyone who spends his entire days in deep introspection. The hatchets and saws need not leave their marks on our souls."

May, 1944 (Iyar, 5704)

NEW VENUE, NEW HOPE

And so we had settled into a routine of prayer, work, study, scrounging for food, staying warm. That last thing was not easy, as our clothing was hardly up to the task, considering the long Siberian winter. All the same, though, sometimes our hunger had to be addressed even at the expense of our insulation. At such times, we actually traded articles of clothing for food. I recalled the Jewish forefather Jacob's request of the Almighty to give him "clothing to wear." One might well ask: Well, what else would one do with clothing? In Siberia I learned the answer. There was another use for clothing – bartering it for something to eat.

In 1944, the Polish government-in-exile struck an agreement with the Soviets to release Polish nationals who had been sent to Siberia. Although for the moment it essentially meant no more than a change of venue for us, we felt – and, as it turned out, rightly – that the move would prove to be the beginning of our liberation from Soviet territory. The authorities transported our group westward to the Caucasus, or Kavkaz. There, too, we were to work on a *kolkhoz*, but the conditions were very much improved. The climate was less harsh and the degree of control over us was noticeably relaxed.

During our many months in Kavkaz, the authorities would show us newsreels about the war, with an emphasis on Nazi atrocities – concentration camps, gas chambers, the machinery and methods by which millions were murdered. We saw the mounds upon mounds of once living, breathing, speaking people now mere corpses waiting to be reduced to ash by crematoria or bulldozed into unmarked mass graves.

I could not help but imagine my parents and siblings among the dead, which – except for my two brothers in Palestine – they likely were. And it was years, many years – even in America where G-d would yet grant me a home and family of my own – before I could take a shower without thinking about the "showers" into which countless soon-to-be-gassed Jews were ordered by Nazi demons in human guise.

But in Kavkaz, even as we began to realize the extent of the devastation to the west, we had no choice but to pay attention, too, to the present and our immediate needs. Using our wits, we managed to engage in some trade. I discovered that with a little work, old discarded motor vehicle tires could be made into a commodity. Having somehow secured a knife, I became quite good at cutting them into pieces suitable for shoe soles, which I bartered for food and other items.

At some point we had gathered enough currency to buy a cow, which was cause for rejoicing. We had not eaten meat for the four years we had been interned in Siberia. The Caucasus was serviced by trains and somehow it was arranged that a *shochet*, a ritual slaughterer, would come to dispatch our cow. He arrived and did his task. But when he inspected some of the animal's inner organs, as Jewish law requires, he discovered it was a *tereifa*, that a lesion or hole in one of its lungs had rendered its meat unkosher.

As high as our hopes for a meat meal had been raised, that was how hard they came crashing down. Our first reaction was imaginable. But, we soon came to realize, we had not persevered through our Siberian years to become depressed by a culinary disappointment. Like everything that had happened to us testified, we had not been abandoned by G-d. He just had different plans for us than we imagined. Maybe, like our ancestors in the Sinai desert, our yearning for meat was evidence that we had not properly appreciated our lot, and the outcome was a lesson in our development for us to ponder. Whatever the reason, though, in time we would be granted meat, and more.

In fact, meat – at least fowl – followed soon enough. We had once again pooled some money and, hoping that we were deserving of a happier outcome, purchased some chickens. The *shochet*, this time, was not sent for but rather one of us was chosen to take the bag of squawking birds on a train to a nearby town where the ritual slaughterer did his work. As the youngest member of our group, I was not expecting to be made the emissary, but for some reason I was.

All went smoothly, at least until the return trip, as I held tight to my bag of birds now still, the bag slowly dripping blood. I had to wait outside the town at the rail tracks for the train that would take me back to where we were living. There was no station, just the tracks, and no one else was there.

Standing there with my leaking bag, I heard the unmistakable sound of wolves howling. I imagined them having picked up the scent of the freshly slaughtered chickens and heading down from the surrounding hills to claim their natural birthright. I knew just what I would do: offer them the birds and head off quickly, empty-handed.

Maybe, I thought further, I should altogether avoid a confrontation and just leave the wolves' dinner for them right then and there for them to claim whenever they were ready to come down from the hills. But no, I thought, I am a trusted messenger, and my friends, having accepted Divine judgment regarding their desire for a piece of cow meat, deserved this first-time-in-years meal of chicken. As I pondered the different scenarios, the train arrived.

When I returned to my friends, they were so happy to see me.

I was even more happy myself.

PART IV

Leaving a Loathsome Land

Spring, 1945 (Nisan, 5705)

A PATH TO FREEDOM THROUGH THE BELLY OF THE BEAST

When the war officially ended, Polish nationals like us were to be repatriated. The darkness that enveloped us in Nizhna Machavaya had lifted somewhat in Kavkaz. Now, actual glimmers of light flickered before our inner eyes. We were boarded onto cattle cars just like those that had brought us to Siberia. This time, though, the doors of the cars were not locked from the outside and we were heading westward, back to Poland. It wasn't where we wanted to go — we knew that the world we had left behind was not there anymore — but we were relieved to be free of Russian authority.

We left Kavkaz in two groups. The first included Rabbi Nekritz and his family; I was part of the second.

This time, the journey, while it took just as long, was more tolerable, buoyed as we were with hope for the future. We may not have known what lay ahead for us, but we knew one thing: it wasn't the frigid Siberian taiga. And for the moment that was more than good enough for us.

The train took us to Lodz, once a large, bustling city, fully a third of whose inhabitants, before the war, had been Jews. The city's Jewish residents, along with other Jews in the vicinity — more than 200,000 souls — had been confined during the early years of the war to a part of the city designated as the Jewish ghetto, separated from the rest of Lodz by wooden barriers and barbed wire. From there, they were sent to concentration camps, where all but several hundred perished.

When we arrived, we saw a scene of destruction. All the city's Jewish landmarks had been demolished.

There was, though, a Jewish organization active there, as elsewhere: the Bricha. Hebrew for "escape" and founded by people like Abba Kovner, a survivor of the Vilna ghetto who was a poet and partisan, the Bricha sought to move Jewish refugees to places where they would be safe. Primarily, it tried to transport Jews by ship to Palestine, but it aided Jews in any way it could. As Germany was occupied by the United States, Great Britain, France and the Soviet Union, the Bricha set itself the task of routing Jews through Poland into the United States-occupied zone of Germany. To get to Berlin's American zone, though, which I and some of my friends decided would be the best destination for us, one had to pass through the city's Soviet zone. So we weren't quite free of the Russians just yet.

We were brought by the Bricha to a city called Stetchin, near the German border. From there we were to be transported to the American zone. We didn't quite understand at the time how that was going to happen. But the Bricha had gotten the transport of refugees down to something of a science. Their operations were oiled by well-placed bribes, to sentries and their superiors guarding important crossing points. Those bribes, we eventually found out, were important parts of the plan for getting us out of the Russian zone. Unfortunately, despite the grease, the machinery didn't always work as smoothly as hoped.

We were placed in a canvas-covered truck and strictly instructed to sit on the floor. There wasn't enough room for that, though, and so many of us, including me, stood instead.

The full account of what happened next we only came to know later. Apparently the truck driver was a Russian hire, and a Bricha man disguised in a Russian officer's uniform sat in the other seat in the truck's cab. We, the cargo, were in the back of the truck, hidden underneath the canvas.

When the truck approached the sentry point, the Bricha representative sensed that something was wrong. Not only were there several motorcycles at the post, unusual in itself, but the guard who was expected to be there — and who had been "convinced" to allow us safe passage — was nowhere to be seen. Another guard had taken his place.

The Bricha man turned to the driver.

"As you approach the sentry point," he said, "slow down and wait until the guard passes in front of the truck to question you. When he does, hit the gas pedal, run him down and proceed at full speed onto the road beyond."

The driver, understandably, expressed some doubts about the plan, but when the Bricha man took out a pistol and held it to the man's head, he had a change of heart.

The truck approached the sentry point and slowed. The guard walked in front of the truck and the vehicle lurched forward, clipping the guard but not incapacitating him. Those of us in the back, who could not see anything and knew nothing of the change in original plan, realized only that the truck had stopped and then accelerated wildly. And that bullets were piercing the canvas walls. And, in the cases of many of us, our flesh.

Even some of those who had been seated low were wounded. I had been standing, my hand tightly grasping one of the metal rafters to which the canvas was fastened. At first, as we had just passed a group of trees, I imagined that the sudden pain in my arm had come from a branch that had somehow entered the back of the truck. The blood that began to run down my arm, the sound of the automatic fire and the cries of my fellow passengers quickly brought me to a different conclusion.

Our planned quick trip to American Berlin was obviously put on hold, and the truck sped on, turning wildly this way and that, until it took a final sharp turn off the road and disgorged its cargo. Our unscheduled stop was a farmhouse.

The family living there provided us some cloth to use as bandages for those who were injured. G-d had protected us; none of us were seriously hurt. The bullet I had taken had gone straight through my arm – and had whizzed past my friend's ear, he later told me. Had I been holding my arm straight rather than in a bent position, I was later told by a doctor, the bullet would likely have shattered the bone rather than just damaged some nerves and tendons. And had my friend's head been an inch to the side of where it was…

I thanked G-d for His mercy.

The way to Berlin now involved a train ride. It was a disappointment not to be delivered "door to door," so to speak, as had been planned. But at least on this train we sat on actual seats, not a cattle-car floor, and our hearts held not dread but hope.

To hide the blood-stained makeshift bandage wrapped around my arm, I donned my Siberian overcoat.

The train trip lasted only a few minutes – at least for me. I had apparently lost enough blood to slip out of consciousness, because it wasn't long after we began rolling along that I found myself awakening – once again – in a hospital.

I had no idea exactly where I was, but soon enough found out that it was Berlin, the American zone. My friends came to visit and explained that the trip had gone safely and after our arrival they had transported me to the hospital where my wound was found to be infected, and that it had now been cleaned and properly bandaged. I was very happy.

I stayed in the hospital for several days, during which time I received therapy to counter the effects of the nerve damage.

When I was released, I had mixed feelings about being in Germany's capital. On the one hand, for the first time since the beginning of the war, I actually felt safe. On the other, I was repulsed to be walking among Germans. I couldn't look a single one of them in the face.

These were, after all, the people who had elected and aided and supported the unspeakable evil that had raged through Europe over the previous six years, the European cataclysm that had consumed my parents and siblings – and millions more of my more distant relatives. Germans on the streets of the city begged for food and cigarettes, and we sensed that the local populace was afraid of the strangers in its midst – American soldiers and refugees alike. I could not help but take some satisfaction from their fear and their humiliation.

To this day, I cannot bring myself to grant a German the same presumption of basic goodness I assume in most people. If he can prove to me that – if he is older – he did not play a part in the Holocaust; or – if he is younger – he is not a Jew-hater, then I can force myself to see him as anyone else. After all, there were Germans who, even during the war and at risk to their lives, helped Jews escape the evil their fellows had forged; and many Germans, and the German government today, have expressed deep shame over what happened over the years before and during the Second World War. But until and unless I am convinced of a German's goodness, I cannot help but imagine a Nazi soul hiding behind his face.

TRANQUILITY IN THE WAKE OF TRIAL

Papers were somehow obtained that allowed us to leave the American zone of Berlin for American-occupied greater Germany. We journeyed to a city named Salzheim, where a good number of Jewish survivors of concentration camps and ghettos were sent. They were the proverbial "charred wood plucked from the fire" of the Holocaust. Those Jews were skin and bones. But then, come to think of it, so was I.

A yeshiva was organized in Salzheim and headed by Rabbi Gershon Kovler, an older student who undertook to provide an environment of Torah-study for students like me.

Reb Gershon, who also came to be known by the surname Leibman, had spent the war years in various concentration camps. Every camp survivor was a miracle but his emergence whole from Buchenwald was particularly remarkable. He was said to have once seen his Nazi guards eating at a table over which they had spread a confiscated *tallis*, or Jewish prayer shawl. Unable to contain himself, he walked over and pulled it out from under their plates and cups. Needless to say, he suffered a terrible beating as a result, but, unlike many a Jew who had been guilty of a much more minor "crime," he was not killed by his imprisoners.

Nor was he punished for — or even caught in — another brazen violation of concentration camp rules. It was told that, late at night, he would infiltrate a room where dead bodies were kept for the next day's cremation, to ensure that all the bodies were in fact lifeless. He apparently had helped resuscitate several such seemingly deceased men whom he returned to their barracks. In one such instance, where an inmate's death had already been recorded (and thus he could not be returned to his own barracks), Reb Gershon brought the "resurrected" man back to his barracks, where Reb Gershon and the others there cared for him, sharing their meager rations with their permanent guest until their liberation.

I would remain in the Salzheim yeshiva from then, the middle of 1945, until 1947, studying in an atmosphere of tranquility. Much of the Torah-study I did in my youth was in Salzheim. Siberia had been an important time of religious growth for all of us who were students of Rabbi Nekritz. And we did much Torah study when we could during our sojourn in the east. But, by necessity, most of our waking hours we spent as workers, usually frozen ones at that. So the opportunities for study, not to mention the necessary texts, were very rare. Salzheim, on the other hand, was an actual yeshiva. Although it was on the cursed soil of Germany, it was in a way a resumption of the months we had spent in Vilna and Birzh. My study there was a revenge of sorts on the Germans, who – whether directly or through their willing partners in evil – had murdered my parents and siblings, aside from the two who had made their way to Palestine.

One of the members of the Salzheim yeshiva was a Rabbi Yaakov Krett. He was particularly expert at the *nussach*, or musical style, of the prayer services of the Jewish holidays. I was musically inclined and soaked up his beautiful rendering of the service for the holidays and Days of Awe. It would come to serve me well for many years to come as a congregational rabbi.

During the time I spent in Salzheim, I established contact with my surviving brothers, and found out that I had a cousin – a Gelchinsky, from my mother's side – in New York. I managed to contact him and he was kind enough to send me a certificate that attested to his willingness to take responsibility for me if the United States allowed me to immigrate. That was a most valuable document, of course, and a very wonderful kindness on his part. In June, 1947, I was cleared to immigrate to the United States. I sailed on the SS Ernie Pyle and arrived at Ellis Island a few weeks later. After being examined and processed, I found myself a new immigrant in New York.

PART V

New World, New Life

FINDING MY FOOTING – AND MY PARTNER

America was truly a new world, a wondrous one. For the first time in my life I felt safe. I and my fellow Jews could practice our religion and no one would bother us. Most Americans were Christians of course, but there was no need to stay indoors during their holidays because of priests' sermons. There were no Nazis setting synagogues aflame. There were no communists, at least not any who were actively seeking to uproot Judaism or exiling Jews to frozen wastelands. This was – and is – a very special country, and I was proud to be part of it, and eventually to become an American citizen.

We refugees were warmly welcomed by the Jews already in the New World, our own new world. Families in effect adopted yeshiva boys who had survived the war years in Europe or, as in our case, Siberia. Beis Yosef, the Novardhoker yeshiva, had been reestablished several years earlier in

Brooklyn and, naturally, I joined – or, better, rejoined – it. The yeshiva had a dormitory and so I had a place not only where I could study but where I could live.

We newcomers did not focus on the past. It sounds strange to many people today that we did not choose then to speak about our experiences during the war years. It sounds strange even to me, now that so many years have passed and I have come to revisit my memories and to share details of those years with others. But at the time we didn't want to remember, only to look forward, to build – families, institutions, ourselves. King Solomon taught us that there is a time for everything. It was a time then for looking ahead, not back.

I used the first $75 I was given, a gift from a Jewish social service organization, to buy a new pair of *tefillin*. Those from my bar mitzvah, which had accompanied me during my journey through Poland, Lithuania, Siberia and Germany, were no longer kosher. The ink on the parchment had crumbled or faded beyond repair. So along with a new life, I had new *tefillin* too.

It was only years later that I found out that the parchment texts in my new *tefillin* — the paragraphs from the Torah that form the heart of the objects — had been written by a second cousin of mine, a scribe in Jerusalem. He was, in fact, the personal scribe of the Gerer Rebbe, one of the most revered Chassidic rabbis in the world. My second cousin shared my name, Simcha Bunim, although he had kept my original surname, Szafranowicz.

Unknown to me, a young woman was working in an office not far from the yeshiva as I resumed my studies. In the same building, by a stroke of Divine fortune, lived Rabbi Krett, who had been in the yeshiva with me in Salzheim. He would come to the Brooklyn Novardhoker yeshiva often, and one day he came over to me and told me that he had a good idea for a *shidduch*, or marriage-match, that he thought I should consider.

"Paitche," or Puah, Kahn, who was known to her American-born friends as Pauline, had come to Baltimore from a Polish town called Drohitzen before the war as a little girl with her parents, two brothers and grandmother. She lost her grandmother Rochel and one of her brothers, Dovid Mordechai, when she was only 14. Dovid Mordechai had been studying in yeshiva in New York when he took ill and, before the seriousness of his sickness was recognized, he had died. His death was a terrible blow to the family, made even more tragic by — and probably contributing to — the death, only two years later, of Paitche's father, Rabbi Noach Kahn. The respected rabbi of a Baltimore congregation, he had been ordained by the famed Rabbi Boruch Ber Leibovitz in Poland, and he was only 48 when he passed on.

Puah's mother, Etkeh, or Esther, who had suffered the loss of her mother, son and husband in so short a time, was a determined woman with a calm, almost regal, bearing, She persevered with dignity and managed to purchase a Jewish bookstore in Baltimore, which she operated along with her surviving son, Moshe, who had joined the American army during the war years, served in the Philippines — surviving an enemy naval attack at one point by clinging to a floating piece of wood for many hours — and then returned home to his mother and sister.

My future mother-in-law would travel back and forth by train to New York regularly, to purchase Jewish books for her store and, before the Sukkos holiday, to choose and bring back the *arba minim*, or "four species" — the citron, palm fronds, myrtle and willow branches used on the holiday.

Paitche, like her mother and brother, was fully committed to the Jewish faith. But there was no Jewish girls' school in Baltimore and so she and her Jewish friends attended public school. During her teenage years, though, along with a group of her friends, she received religious tutelage from, and had a close relationship with, the famed Rabbi Shimon Schwab, who at that time was a congregational rabbi in Baltimore.

I told Rabbi Krett that yes, I would be most interested in meeting the young lady he thought would make a good match for me, and he arranged a "date." We rode New York's subways and took walks together. We spoke in Yiddish. It was the spoken language in her home and I hadn't yet learned to speak English. There wasn't much for an observant couple to do but I shared some of the Yiddish songs that we had sung in yeshiva, and she seemed to enjoy listening to me.

An audiofile of Rabbi Shafran singing the song below in Yiddish can be obtained by emailing hashgachapress@gmail.com with "Vander Leid" in the subject box.

Vander Leid ("Wander-Song")

[translated from the Yiddish]

I wander far, from land to land,
My wander-stick tight in my hand;
Over mountains, over vale,
Seeking out my kin Yisrael;
Over mountains, over vale,
Seeking out my kin Yisrael

Persecuted, nowhere to stay,
From every host-land, cast away;
Sent to the stake, condemned to die,
"Shma Yisrael" the final cry;
Sent to the stake, condemned to die,
"Shma Yisrael" the final cry;

Worn and tired, it's been so long;
All that's left is my wander-song,
To give me pride that I'm a Jew;
Jewish People, I come to you.

To give me pride that I'm a Jew;
Jewish People, I come to you.

A Temple stood once; now we're bereft,
A defiant wall is all that's left;
Amid endless tears there, a vow anew:
"I have never forgotten you."
Amid endless tears there, a vow anew:
"I have never forgotten you."

Wailing at that survivor-wall,
Pining to return one day, strong and tall,
In the distance, a voice sublime:
"Two thousand years, yes, it is time."
In the distance, a voice sublime:
"Two thousand years, yes, it is time."

Enough wandering; End our night;
Shine upon us Your holy light;
Remove the wander-stick from my hand;
Lead me to our fathers' land.
Remove the wander-stick from my hand;
Lead me to our fathers' land.

March, 1949 (Adar, 5709)

LAYING ROOTS, LEARNING A LANDSCAPE

Although Paitche and I had been born in the same country, indeed the same region of pre-war Poland, we were very different. She had been living in America since her early childhood and, although fully committed to her Jewish religious obligations, felt very much "at home" in her adopted country. English had become her first language (even as she remained fluent in the Yiddish spoken by her family) and she knew things about America that I had not yet learned. And I was a new immigrant whose life revolved around the yeshiva, just beginning to learn English and without any close family nearby.

Even so, we came to realize that our differences made us a complementary couple and, with her mother's and brother's blessings, we decided to marry. I didn't realize it at the time, but I later found out that my future mother-in-law had sold a valuable investment in order to pay for our wedding. We were married by Rabbi Yaakov Yitzchok Ruderman, the Rosh Yeshiva, or dean, of the Ner Israel Rabbinical College in Baltimore (whose daughter Chana, eventually Rebbetzin Chana Weinberg, was one of my new wife's closest friends); and our first post-wedding Sheva Brachos celebration was in Rabbi Schwab's home.

We returned as a couple to New York, where I studied at the East New York Lomzher Kollel, a Torah-study institution for married men. I became a United States citizen and took on the Americanized name Shafran.

But we didn't remain in New York for very long. Expecting our first child, we moved to Baltimore at the end of 1949. I took a job teaching religious studies at the Yeshivas Chofetz Chaim, also known as Talmudical Academy (and informally as "T.A."), a local boys' yeshiva where I was fortunate to remain for four years. Among my students were more than a few who went on to become great scholars and leaders of yeshivos. I don't credit myself with having played any role in their later accomplishments, but I do feel fortunate to have been a small part of their young lives.

My wife worked as a secretary in an office and in 1950 our first child, Rochel, was born. In 1952, I found a position in a small synagogue, Adath Yeshurun, which was known as the Shadover Shul. Until my arrival, the shul, on Pimlico Road, had had no steady rabbi; one or another rabbi would be employed each fall just to lead services for the High Holidays. I continued to teach at TA while I led services and classes in Talmud for the mostly elderly congregants and, on the Sabbath, delivered a sermon as well.

I composed and delivered my sermons in Yiddish at first, but when more non-Yiddish speakers came to join the shul, my wife would help me translate my words into proper English. I had attended an English class for immigrants at night and picked up a good deal of the language, but I was still learning; and my wife, who spoke unaccented English (well, a little Southern accented, as was common in Baltimore – or Bawlmur, as locals pronounced it), became my real teacher.

She would carefully type her English translations of my sermons on index cards, which I would use when delivering them, always knowing that the result was really the product of a joint effort. Eventually, I felt more comfortable with English, and increasingly uncomfortable reading my sermons instead of delivering them directly from my heart. And so I took the leap and began to speak without any written aids, and have done so ever since.

Over the decade and a half during which the shul functioned in that location, my wife was as busy as I was with shul responsibilities. I may have conducted services and delivered sermons, but she undertook to buy and cook food for the Kiddush repast after Shabbos services; and on Shabbos afternoons she conducted a special program – an "*oneg Shabbos*," or "Sabbath enjoyment" – for congregants' young children. She would tell the little boys and girls stories, teach them songs, and offer them refreshments. My wife and I were truly a team.

Rochel (Shafran) Zoberman:

Today, when "kiruv," or outreach, groups that help Jews get closer to the Jewish faith are plentiful and successful, it is hard to imagine that there was a time in America when the word "kiruv" and the phrase "Jewish outreach" had not been heard.

That was the case when I was growing up, in the 1950s and 1960s. But the effort existed. I know, because my mother ran what anyone today would call a weekly kiruv program for the Jewish children in our neighborhood.

Some were the children of congregants of my father's shul but others were just local Jewish kids. Whenever my mother or my father would meet a Jewish child or a Jewish parent, they would extend an invitation for the child to attend the weekly "Oneg Shabbos" or "Enjoyment of Shabbos" gathering. Today it might be called a "kumzitz."

Mama, who had never been trained, or ever worked professionally as a teacher, would energetically lead the children in singing, tell them stories and offer them candies and baked goods she would bring to the shul before Shabbos.

I, and later my brother Avi, would accompany her. We were somewhat different, we realized, from the other children in attendance. Few if any of them came from religiously observant homes. But for that hour each Shabbos, they tasted the spirit of the holy day, and learned something about their heritage.

We may not have called it that, but an early kiruv group is just what it was. I don't know what happened to those children, who might certainly be grandparents today. I wonder if any of them or their children shunned intermarriage, keep kosher homes, observe the Sabbath. . . became fully observant. Did the

seeds my mother planted in their heads and hearts when they were little take root and grow? In my imagination — and I hope in fact — they did. How could they not?

Over that period, I made it a point to continue my own Torah studies, and would regularly go to the Ner Israel yeshiva to hear Torah lectures from Rabbi Ruderman.

We had moved from the apartment we had been renting and, for about three years, lived in the attic of the shul. In 1954, our second child, Avrohom Yitzchak, or Avi, was born; he was named after my father. During those years, I made an effort to bring some younger members into the shul and, thank G-d, was successful convincing several Jewish families in the neighborhood – known as Lower Park Heights (then a hub of Jewish Baltimore, today a no-man's-land) – to join it. Some were Sabbath-observant, but others were not. I tried to raise the religious commitment of all of the shul's members, something that was appreciated by many but, as might be expected, not by all.

The same was true about the *mechitza*, or partition between the men's and women's sections of the sanctuary, that I had installed in the shul. I was perfectly willing to accept any congregant, observant or not, on his or her own terms. I understood how very different America was from the *shtetl* where I came of age – how this new land was so very distant in more than just miles from pre-war Poland. But Jewish standards had to remain the ideal to which I encouraged the congregants to strive – and Jewish standards would certainly determine how the shul would operate. Those who sought a place of worship that didn't consider itself bound by Jewish law always had other options.

And so, while I spoke regularly not only about the week's Torah reading but also about the importance of honoring the Sabbath and holidays, among those who were in attendance were some who had driven cars to come to shul. I did not bar them from coming, but it was a wonderful victory when – as happened a number of times over the years – someone either moved closer to the shul to avoid having to drive, or walked a long distance to attend services, or stopped attending services in our shul so that they could attend a shul within walking distance of their homes.

But there were many others who could not bring themselves to undertake Sabbath-observance. One man who for a long while lived only several blocks from the shul moved to another neighborhood far away but maintained his membership in the shul. Before the High Holidays of the year he moved away, he told me that there was no shul near where he now lived and that since it was so far away he would have to drive to shul to join us.

"Are you asking me or telling me?" I asked.

After a moment's thought, he replied, "Asking."

"In that case, take a *machzor*," I said, referring to a prayer book for the holidays and offering him one of the shul's, "and please pray at home."

When Rosh Hashana morning arrived, though, he was in shul. I knew he had driven his car and was disappointed. But I could not prevent him from joining the services. In America, I had learned, one had to be a patient guide. It was important to stand on principle but also to be understanding of others at whatever place they were. And one had to be prepared for disappointments.

Avi Shafran:

A few years before I became bar-mitzvah, I began to accompany my father to shul each morning, which meant arising very early. To this day I don't know if my being an "early morning person" is part of my physiological makeup or the result of my routine of those formative years. Whichever it is, I find it fairly easy to arise before most of the world (and compelled, similarly, to retire at night earlier than many people), I think most clearly when the sun has yet to reveal itself and I am filled with energy when others are seeking it in a cup of strong coffee.

Those childhood mornings still retain their glow. Despite my age and size, I was part of an adult fraternity — the shul-goers of Pimlico Road. And the men who made up the minyan — all of whom I thought of as very old, although they represented pretty much every age group — seemed to regard me as one of their own. Or, at least, that's what I imagined.

In the winter, we would leave the house, bundled against the cold, as stars were still shining brightly in the clear, dark sky. In the summer, only the birds stirred as we walked to the car. In all seasons, we would drive a round-about route to the shul, picking up at least one, sometimes two, passengers at an exact appointed time.

One, I remember, was an elderly and frail man. He had a scholarly demeanor and I imagine he was indeed a learned man. But he was a very quiet one, so I have only the imagining. What I know, though, is that he was dedicated and prompt, always standing in front of his house when we came by on the way to shul. I sat in the back seat and at some point took over my father's privilege of getting out to open the front passenger door for him.

The other regular "pick-up", at least for a year or two, was a blind man. My father, and later I, would guide him from his porch or doorway, down the sidewalk to the car.

As little boys like to do, I would find ways of entertaining myself in the back seat during the interminable — it might have been ten full minutes — trip to shul each morning. Once, running the edge of a toy across the fabric at the back of the seat in front of me, the seat where the blind man sat, I saw him give a start.

"What was that?" he exclaimed, and I honestly had no idea what he was referring to. My father, though, later guessed that I had generated some sudden noise, a good description of my scratching the seat fabric.

"When a person loses one of his senses," my father explained to me, "sometimes other senses become sharper." Our passenger, he theorized, lacking his sight, may have been particularly well-tuned to sounds, hearing them more loudly than we do.

I was too curious to not test the theory, and on future occasions made various disturbances of the quiet in my back seat laboratory, watching our passenger for indications that I had startled him. I am ashamed to admit that my experiments yielded positive data, seeming to support — at least for my sample, one blind man — my father's theory. Once the data were in, though, I desisted from further experimentation, and tried to stay perfectly still throughout the ride to shul. I feel shame today for playing junior scientist those days.

MICROPHONES, MOTHERS, AND MAMZERUS

There were many challenges, some easier, some harder. It wasn't terribly difficult, for instance, to say no to the congregant – a neighbor of ours – who insisted that the shul install a microphone in the sanctuary for use on Shabbos and holidays when services were well attended. There was nothing to speak about. I told him it would be a violation of the Sabbath. He threatened to leave the shul. I told him I hoped he wouldn't but the Sabbath laws weren't negotiable. He left. The world didn't end.

It was much harder to face the mother of a young woman who was about to be married and who had asked me to officiate at the wedding. As was my practice, I asked a number of questions, to make sure there were no Jewish law, or *halachic*, problems in the couple marrying. When I asked the mother if there were any divorces in the immediate family, she was quiet for a moment and then began to cry.

She told me that, yes, she herself had been divorced, and that her daughter, the bride, was the offspring of her and her new husband.

"Was there a Jewish divorce?" I asked, since the transfer of a carefully prepared divorce document was essential to the dissolving of the first marriage.

"No," she answered. "My first husband abandoned me and we were never in touch again."

That was a terrible problem. It meant that her second marriage was a forbidden one, as she was still, no matter what she or the state thought, married to her first husband when she married her second one. That would make the children of her second marriage – including the bride – *mamzerim*, or Jews who are permitted to marry only other similar products of forbidden marriages or converts. Her daughter's groom was neither.

I didn't render a decision right away. There was still some hope that the situation might be salvaged and the taint of *mamzerus* avoided for her children. If the woman's first wedding had been conducted in a non-*halachic* way – if, perhaps, the witnesses to the ceremony had been unqualified for any of a number of reasons – then the woman's first marriage, according to respected authorities, would have been null and void from the start, and no divorce would have been needed to end it. In that case, her daughter would carry no *halachic* stigma at all, and be permitted to marry her intended.

I asked the mother who the presiding rabbi had been at her first marriage. When she told me his name – he was a fine and upstanding Orthodox rabbi who I knew would have insisted on the highest standards for the wedding ceremony – my heart sank.

I had to tell her I couldn't perform the ceremony because I couldn't sanction the marriage.

It was a very hard thing to say, but it had to be said. It was like a doctor telling a patient bad news. Pretending things weren't so wouldn't change the facts.

I think she found a clergyman to perform the wedding, and she left our shul. But I did what I had to do, and she heard what she had to hear, whether she accepted it or not.

---

c. 1960 (5720)

Rochel (Shafran) Zoberman:

The family car was a special place for us children. With our father usually at the wheel, it took us to school, on trips and to friends' homes for visits. Sometimes it even took us in a circle – like when Baltimore's Beltway was first opened for traffic -- when the car trip was just for the fun of the drive. Today's cars are more safe and comfortable, but there were many good times experienced in seatbelt-less Fords and Chevys whose "air conditioning" consisted of open windows. The roar of the air didn't allow for conversation and the wind-tunnel effect made for a blizzard of hair and yarmulkes, kerchiefs and hats. Wild, fun times.

One car trip, though, I recall with a shiver. It was terrifying.

It was Purim, always a happy and busy day, and one filled with delivering mishloach manos, the customary gifts of food to friends. My brother Avi and I were in the back seat of the

family Chevy II (or maybe the hippopotamus-like Plymouth that preceded it) as our father drove to the Ner Yisroel yeshiva, which today is a sprawling campus — really a small, beautiful town — but was then a single building in a neighborhood known as Forest Park.

I don't know if we were delivering mishloach manos to students there or to the Rosh Yeshiva or other faculty members. What I do know is that when we pulled up to the yeshiva building, we saw students looking out of second-floor windows, several lower windows shattered and a group of clearly non-yeshiva-student boys throwing the last of their rocks at unbroken panes before making their getaway on foot.

Tata didn't stop the car. He swung it around in the direction of the fugitives and gave chase. Avi and I were tossed around in the back as the car lurched this way and that, making sharp turns and speeding all the while. My brother remembers the experience as fun (he was a boy, of course); my recollection is more terror-tinged. Neither of us (nor our father) can remember if we caught any of the culprits, but they must have experienced some fear of their own to have a car chase them so relentlessly.

At the time I think I wondered why our father thought it was important to give chase. Thinking back now, though, I easily imagine him thinking about the fact that in the old country Jews were subject to insult and violence about which they could do nothing at all. Here in America, though, a Jew could actually pursue a criminal. And so, why wouldn't he?

We went back to the yeshiva at some point. Police had arrived and filled out their report; in his recollection, Avi sees a culprit or two being arrested, but isn't sure if it's true recall or a wishful manufactured memory. Neither of us remembers the delivery of our holiday packages, but that must have eventually happened.

A TRIP ONCE UNDREAMED OF

B y 1961, when our third child Noach was born, we had saved enough to make a down payment on a small house not far from the shul, on a street called Virginia Avenue. I let my wife decide whether the house itself was suitable. If it was for her, it was for me. The main thing that concerned me – and would always be the first thing I looked for whenever we moved – was whether there was a good place to put a *sukkah*. There was a small back yard behind this house, though, and so I was happy that my wife liked the house.

Our neighbors, most of them Jewish, were very welcoming and friendly. Some of them even belonged to my shul. One couple, the Waranches, were regulars at the shul and cared much about us. When my family and I went away for a few days one summer in the early sixties, we returned to find a concrete patio in our backyard – a gift from the Waranches, who knew how much our *sukkah* meant to us and how messy it was when it rained on the holiday and the table and chairs sank into the muddy grass. That was a truly thoughtful gift.

The year Noach was born, I was also able to do something I had dreamed of doing ever since the end of the war: travel to Israel to see my two surviving brothers for the first time in so many, so eventful years.

My wife did not feel it would be right for her to leave our children behind – Noach was, after all, only a few months old – so she encouraged me to make the trip without her. Her mother, though, also wanted to visit the Holy Land, and so my mother-in-law and I ended up making the trip together. She turned out to be as adventurous as I was, even taking a small propeller plane with me to Eilat, at Israel's southern tip.

I remember deeply wanting to see Kever Rochel, the site revered as the burial place of Jacob's wife Rachel. It is a holy site with much religious significance. These days, it is regularly visited by Jews in Israel, but then it was still under Jordanian control and off limits to Jews. I heard, though, that a certain Jerusalem bus took tourists to a hilltop outside the city from which Kever Rochel could be seen in the distance. I found out which bus it was and took it to the top of the hill.

Peering through binoculars that had been mounted there, I gazed at the domed building that I had known about and dreamed about but never knew if I would ever see. I must have spent some time with those binoculars and with my thoughts, because when I finally tore myself away, I saw that the bus had left on its return trip. I had to hitchhike a ride back to Jerusalem.

A car filled with Jewish people stopped for me and I managed to cram myself in. It wasn't a very comfortable ride and I marveled at the "kindness of strangers" the driver and occupants had shown. But then I realized it was really the kindness of family.

In later years, I would make other trips to the Holy Land with my wife. That first one, though, even without her, was especially memorable. Not only was it a way to thank my mother-in-law for letting me marry her daughter (and sacrificing so much, as I later realized, to make the wedding) but because it was, at least for what was left of the Shafranowiczes, a family reunion.

My brother Nachman had been one of the founders of a kibbutz, Ein Hashofet, in the northern Israeli region of Ramat Menashe, not far from Haifa. Its name means "Spring of the Judge" and the jurist to whom it refers was United States Supreme Court Louis Brandeis, who was alive when it was named in his honor. Nachman had been one of the builders of the kibbutz, a pioneer in every sense of the word, and was very respected among the residents of Ein Hashofet.

It was not a religious kibbutz; in fact it was affiliated with the staunchly secular, socialist Hashomer Hatzair movement. But although Nachman had not retained the religious observance of his upbringing, he had no negative feelings toward Jewish belief or observance. The circumstances of his life had simply allowed him to drift from them. When I first saw him again on that trip, it was a very emotional moment. We were not a rabbi and a kibbutznik but simply two brothers who had been separated almost 30 years earlier and who, in the interim, had lost brothers, sisters and parents.

After we embraced and wiped away our tears, I remember asking him, only half in jest, what had happened to him, why he had shrunk! Of course, the last time I had seen him before that meeting I had been a small child and he, a teen-ager, had towered over me. I shouldn't have expected to have to crane my neck again to see his face, but somehow looking straight ahead and seeing his joyous eyes and broad smile surprised me.

During our trip to Israel, my mother-in-law and I stayed with my other surviving brother, Chaim Meir, with whom I had a similarly heartfelt re-union. Joining us for a day there was one of Nachman's sons, Gilad, who was on leave from army service. He and I slept in the same room. Having just met for the first time, we had a long uncle-nephew conversation, about many things.

At one point, I remember discussing the Jewish right to Eretz Yisrael, the Holy Land. I asked Gilad, who had been raised on Ein Hashofet, what he con-sidered to be the source of that right.

"It's the same right the French have to France," he replied.

"But," I pointed out, "the Arabs claim the same right on those grounds to the same land."

He didn't have an answer to that, and so I told him what I believed, that the Torah had deeded us the Land, and was our only true justification for being there. The fact that the Torah begins with the account of the creation of the world, explains Rashi, the prime commentary on the Five Books of Moses, is to counter the claims of the "seven nations" – those peoples who populated the Holy Land before the Jews conquered it after the Exodus – that the Holy Land is theirs. The Torah makes clear from the very start that "the entire earth is G-d's; He created it and He gave [the Holy Land] to whom he wished [at first]; then He purposefully took it from them and gave it to us [the Jews, as the Torah describes]."

The Arabs, in any event, trace their ancestry not to any of the "seven na-tions," but rather to Yishmael, Abraham's son. Their claim to the Land is even weaker, as they only came to live on it many years after the Jews had possessed it and established a kingdom on it. When we were exiled from the land, popula-tions from Arabia and nearer lands became the land's occupiers.

I don't remember if I told my nephew about the claim the Talmud says was lodged over 2000 years ago by descendants of Yishmael (Hagar's son) and those of Ketura (Abraham's second wife) against the Jewish right to the Holy Land – in a world court presided over by Alexander the Great. Since they were descended, no less than the Jews, from Abraham, to whom the Land was promised, the complainants claimed they had just as much a right to it as the Jews.

The representative of the Jews, however, a man called Geviha ben Psisa, asked the Arab representatives for the source of their claim. "The Torah," they responded.

"If so," Geviha responded, "I too will invoke the Torah, which says that Abraham gave 'all that was his to Yitzchak (Isaac); and to the children of his other wives he gave gifts, and he sent them away from Yitzchak his son... eastward'" (Genesis, 25:5, 6).

July, 1971 (Tammuz, 5731)

The two boys sat on a hill overlooking a valley near the kibbutz. It was the dusk of a summer evening. One had been born and bred on the kibbutz, Ein Hashofet, the son of one of its Polish-born founders, who had immigrated before World War II; the other was an American newcomer to the Holy Land — whose father, the younger brother of the other boy's father, had spent the war years in Siberia with a contingent of fellow students from the Novardhok yeshiva. The American was visiting before the start of his Jerusalem yeshiva's academic term. The cousins had first met only days earlier.

Although their lives were very different, they found sundry things they had in common, born of their connection as young men, as relatives, and, of course, as Jews. At one point the observant boy mentioned in passing the imminence of the Jewish fast day Tisha B'Av.

"We don't observe that on the kibbutz," his cousin pointed out. "The Temple's destruction isn't really relevant to our lives here."

The American boy hesitated a moment before asking, "Do you observe any Jewish day of mourning?"

"Yes," came the reply. "Yom HaShoah."

Another pause, this one even longer. The yeshiva student knew that Tisha B'Av is the national day of Jewish mourning — that it encompasses many a tragedy — in a sense, every tragedy — in Jewish history. Not only were both Jewish Holy Temples destroyed on that day but the rebel Jewish forces at Betar were annihilated by the Romans, several decades after the Second Temple's destruction, on Tisha B'Av as well.

He knew, too, that the expulsion of Jews from England in 1290 C.E., and from France in 1306 C.E. and from Spain in 1492 C.E. all took place on Tisha B'Av as well. He also knew that on Tisha B'Av, 1914, Germany declared war on Russia, turning a regional European conflict into what came to be known as World War I, arguably the genesis of what would culminate, two and a half decades later, in Germany's "Final Solution." But somehow it didn't seem the right time for history lessons.

So, instead, he asked his cousin, "Is your commemoration of the Holocaust important to you?"

"Absolutely," came the reply. "The Holocaust underlies our very identity as Israelis and as Jews."

The American weighed the wisdom of saying what he wanted, and then decided the blood-bond was strong enough to handle it.

"Will you expect your children to pay its memory the same

respect that you do?"

"Of course."

"To feel the same sorrow, to have the same determination to remember that you feel?"

"Of course," the Israeli replied. "My generation will see to it that our children recognize the importance of the Holocaust, how it defines their identity, how important it must continue to be to all Jews."

"And will you expect them, in turn, to transmit the same conviction to their own children — and theirs to theirs?"

"Absolutely. Forever. It is that important."

The American swallowed hard, then spoke.

"As important as the earlier attempts to destroy our people and its faith were to our own ancestors — the events we commemorate and mourn on Tisha B'Av."

Nothing else was said for the moment. The two young men walked back to the kibbutz in silence.

1966 (5726)

MOVING UP, MOVING ON

Neighborhoods change, and as the 1960s progressed, the Jews in ours began to move to more suburban areas, and African-Americans bought their homes. The new neighbors were generally friendly, even if our practices sometimes left them bewildered.

I remember how, shortly before Yom Kippur, one neighborhood boy who had heard something about the holiest day of the Jewish year stopped me on the street and asked me if it was really true that we would be fasting an entire night and all the following day. I confirmed what he had heard and took the opportunity as what they call a "teaching moment" in schools today.

"If a person believes in something strongly enough," I told him, "nothing is too hard."

Other questions from the newcomers to the area were a little harder to answer. Our boys had become friendly with some of the black children and our son Avi would often bicycle around the neighborhood with a neighborhood boy named Junie. One fall day, as they passed the shul, Junie looked at the sign advertising "High Holiday Seats Now Being Sold" and asked Avi, amazed, "You gotta *pay* to *pray* ?" Avi wasn't sure how to respond and so he didn't. When he recounted the conversation to me, I explained a little about the economics of how a shul stays afloat.

I had learned a little myself about the economics of how a family stays afloat. Although the shul was small, its building upkeep, utilities and other expenses didn't allow for a rabbi's salary on which I could raise our family, and my wife wanted to be at home with Noach — as I wanted her to be, too. So, even as

I served the shul – and there were not only services and sermons but, of course, the counseling and hospital visits, weddings and funerals that are part of every rabbi's responsibilities – I found the time to attend night school toward an accounting degree.

It took several years of night classes at the University of Baltimore, but I did eventually receive the degree, thank G-d, and was able to supplement my shul income with a salary from the city of Baltimore, for which I worked as an auditor. It was a job that I took seriously and felt good about – over my years of reviewing contracts and identifying irregularities and fraud I helped save the city a large sum of money. But even so, and even though my income came largely from my city job, the shul was my real "professional" life, and not only in terms of my personal feelings, but in terms of priorities too. There were many days that I had to take off from work because of pressing shul members' needs. But my employer was understanding, and I managed to juggle it all with G-d's help.

Even though the newcomers to the neighborhood and we got along well, and they came to learn much about Judaism from living near our family, they were, all said and done, not Jewish, not the "family" we wanted to live among. And so the transformation of the area made it necessary for the shul to look for a new location. And, as a result, for us to do the same.

We moved first to a rented house at the edge of the most vibrantly Jewish Baltimore neighborhood, Park Heights. Our plan was to wait until the shul found an area in which to relocate and then we would buy a house nearby with the proceeds of the sale of our first home. Our rented house, where we stayed for just about a year, was about a mile and a half from the shul.

There were still a few Jewish people living near the shul and so during the week, I would drive – we had managed to buy a car by then too – there to hold the daily services each morning and evening. On Fridays, I would drive to the shul and walk home after Shabbos evening services, and then walk back and forth on Shabbos morning, and then make the trip again for Shabbos afternoon services and to eat the Shalosh Seudos – the Sabbath late afternoon meal – with the congregants in attendance. My son Avi, a 12-year-old at the time, generally attended services at shuls closer to where we lived that year but he would often accompany me on my final walk to the shul each Shabbos for afternoon services. When Shabbos was over, we would drive home.

Avi Shafran:

My father didn't know it at the time, but I dreaded the walks to and from the old shul when our family lived far from it. The route took us through a rough neighborhood, and on the occasion when I accompanied my father on Shabbos afternoons, I would be shocked to see the sort of ugly behavior that human beings could exhibit. My own non-Jewish friends had always been decent, and so it was deeply disturbing for me to see young people who were very different.

Instead of spending their time doing something constructive, or just watching television, they chose instead to sit on their porches and lunge at each other, fighting and screaming like madmen. And when my father and I would walk by — he in a suit and hat, and I with a yarmulke on my head — they would often hurl anti-Jewish invective our way, at times even pretend to move toward us in a threatening way. My father told me to just ignore them, and I tried. But I still dreaded the thought of those treks, and felt guilty — not that I would have been much help had the locals decided to attack — about not accompanying my father more often.

FAMILY TIES, OLD AND NEW

The last year the shul functioned in its Pimlico Road location saw my son Avi become a bar mitzvah. My brother Chaim Meir traveled from Israel to celebrate the happy occasion with us, which made me feel very good. Life after World War II would never be "normal," but the facts that I had been able to visit my brothers and their families several years earlier, that my brother Nachman and his wife and a daughter had visited me and mine, and now Chaim was visiting made it feel like pieces of our lives' puzzle were somehow coming together.

Even though Chaim had left Europe for Palestine as a young man and was not as observant as we were, he was well familiar with Jewish observance and, of course, spoke Yiddish fluently. That made for a friendly and smooth interaction between him and my mother-in-law. Although Paitche's mother was a meticulously religious woman, she was able to relate to Chaim easily, despite their very different lives.

In fact, on the Shabbos of the bar mitzvah, my son and I made the long walk from the house we were renting in Park Heights to the shul early in the morning, so that Avi could catch his breath and perhaps practice his Torah-reading one more time before services began. My wife and other children came a bit later, and my mother-in-law and brother were to walk together a little later still.

Services had progressed to the point of the Torah reading, though, and there was no sign of Chaim or my mother-in-law. We began to worry, wondering if something had, G-d forbid, happened to them. Eventually, though, they turned up. They had become so engrossed in conversation that they walked well past where they had to turn to reach the shul, and it was only when they had walked close to an hour beyond where they should have turned to reach the shul that they realized they had far overshot their mark.

When they finally arrived and we heard what happened, our anxiety turned to laughter.

Avi Shafran:

There were so many special things I remember about the Shabbos table when I was a boy. There were often — actually usually — guests present, and the food, of course, was imbued with the delicious taste of the Sabbath itself. There were discussions of the parsha, or week's Torah portion, and about other Jewish topics, and my father particularly delighted in asking us riddles from a set of small white soft-cover Hebrew books that he had bought in Israel. The riddles were quite clever and challenging, and they laid the groundwork for simple

sketches of scenes having to do with the parsha that I would prepare for my own small children decades later. Those "parsha pictures", which I still prepare (now, for grandchildren too), in turn, helped inspire my father to fax his children and grandchildren (and many others who have caught wind of his efforts) lists of questions and answers regarding the weekly parsha, culled from a variety of sources. In fact, he published a first volume of such questions and answers, entitled "Ma'adanei Simcha," or "The Delights of Simcha."

Perhaps most memorable from the Shafran Shabbos table in the 1960s and 1970s, when I was among those seated around it, were the stories my father would tell. They weren't true stories, in the sense of historically accurate vignettes, but rather true stories — stories, that is, about truths.

One was about a Polish Jewish peasant who owed a powerful landowner, or poritz, a good sum of money:

The poritz owned a bear cub and mockingly told Mushkeh that the debt would be forgiven if Mushkeh could teach a bear how to pray.

So Mushkeh takes the bear's leash and hands him a siddur, or prayer-book, on whose cover he has placed a drop of honey — as he has on each of the pages of the book. The bear wipes up the first drop of honey with its paw and puts it on his tongue. He's happy, and he wonders of there might be more honey inside. So he opens the book and finds more to eat.

The next day, Mushkeh gives the bear the same siddur, but this time there's honey on every other page. The bear isn't as happy but turns the pages and finds the honey.

Then, the next day, Mushkeh puts honey on only a few of the siddur's pages. Mmmrrrgrrrhhummm, the bear grumbles when he turns pages and finds no honey. He keeps turning the pages, though, and when he finds a drop of honey he wipes it off the page and puts it in his mouth. Mmmmmrrrgrhhummm, he mumbles, turns a few pages quickly, touches one, puts his paw to his mouth and then, Mmmmmrrrgrhhummm again.

So now Mushkeh is ready. He goes to the poritz and says "I have taught the bear how to pray." The poritz doesn't believe him and so Mushkeh shows him. He hands the bear the siddur and the bear opens it, turns a few pages, murmuring mmmm-mmrrgrhhummm as he does, then he stops a minute to lick his finger before turning some more pages and then mmmmmmrrrgrhhummm-ing some more.

The poritz shouts, "That's not praying!"

"Come with me," says Mushkeh, and he takes the poritz to the local shul. They're davening Shacharis and Mushkeh opens the door. And the poritz looks at a shul full of congregants doing just what the bear was doing — murmuring and turning pages! So the poritz has to forgive the debt.

The story, as my father told it, was hilarious. His bear-grumbling was flawless. And the message of the story — what prayer isn't supposed to be — was clear.

Another Shabbos table story that I remember well was told when, in that week's Torah-reading, the prime commentary Rashi wrote "I don't know" about why something in the Torah's text appears the way it does:

A learned galach — *a priest* — *convinced the governor of a European village to expel the town's Jews unless one of them can best the priest in a contest about Biblical words.*

"Tell them to have their greatest scholar meet me on the bridge tomorrow at noon. Each of us will have a heavy weight tied to his foot, and the first one who is stumped by the other one's question on the Torah, Talmud or commentaries will be thrown into the river below."

The governor likes the idea and tells the Jews they have to send somebody to face the galach *on the bridge. Otherwise, they will be expelled from the town.*

So the Jews sit together and they're scared. They know the galach *has studied the Torah a lot. "What if he knows more than any of us?" They wonder who they can send to the bridge the next day to represent them. Nobody volunteers.*

And so, in the manner of Jews in times of crisis, they pray and recite Tehillim. Suddenly, though, their loud beseeching are interrupted by Shmiel the water-carrier, who strides into the room and announces: "I'll do it." He was just a water-carrier, not very learned. But he's confident, and no one else wants to go, so the Jews decide to send him.

The next day at noon, Shmiel and the galach *go up on the bridge and the governor puts a heavy weight on the foot of each of the men. The people of the town, the Jews and the non-Jews, all crowd around on the banks of the river and listen to the contest.*

The galach — *it was only the right thing to do, since the contest was his idea and Shmiel didn't look very threatening* — *offers the Yid the first shot. Shmiel clears his throat and shouts so that everyone can hear. "What does 'aini yode'ah' mean?"*

The galach *answers in a second, and gives the right answer: "I do not know!" The crowd gasps when they hear the words and, before the* galach *can say anything else, Shmiel looks down at the crowd with a look of triumph and indicates to the judges that the* galach *should be thrown off the bridge. They had indeed heard his words and, before the priest could protest, he was unceremoniously cast into the water.*

The Jews are beside themselves with happiness and the non-Jews, among them the governor, wonder what went wrong.

Back at the shtetl town hall, everyone congratulates Shmiel for being so clever. "How did you come up with so brilliant an idea?" they ask.

Shmiel modestly tells them that it wasn't really hard at all. "I was reading Rashi and the 'teitch' — the Yiddish translation of his commentary — and when I saw the words 'aini yode'ah' in Rashi I didn't know what they meant. So I looked at the teitch and saw, in Yiddish, the words 'I don't know'."

"So I figured," Shmiel tells the others, "if the holy ' teitch' didn't know what the words meant, there was no way on earth some galach *would!"*

Rochel (Shafran) Zoberman:

It's funny how small things from childhood can have an effect on how we do things as adults. In my decades teaching at a Bais Yaakov, one of the learning methods I enjoy most (and think my students do, too) is presenting riddles based on the Torah texts we study. It seems an obvious thing to do, but I don't think it would have occurred to me had it not been for the riddle books my father would use to challenge us at the Shabbos table. I don't know who compiled the books, and they seem to have disappeared. But they made an impression on us.

The Torah isn't a game, of course; and a riddle, in a way, is. But being forced to think about the Torah's narratives and laws in different ways, from unusual angles, can be not only enticing to a child but the beginning of something bigger, a deeper valuing of what is being learned, and even a deeper understanding of it.

From the Introduction to *"Ma'adanei Simcha"*:

For several years I wanted to prepare questions on the weekly Torah portion read in synagogue. And when I saw that my son Avi had drawn pictures on the portion for his young children to guess what they depicted and become involved in the verses, I decided to undertake the question-and-answer format.

As I would study various books on the Torah, when I would come across something interesting but not too complex, I would turn the thought into a question and answer.

As first I sent the results to my children and grandchildren and to various members of my shul who were interested in receiving copies of the weekly sheets. Then, as I spent several hours daily studying in the Ner Israel yeshiva's study hall, several of the students studying there also requested copies, which I was

happy to provide them, on the condition that they use them at their Shabbos meals.

I have cited the source for each question and answer (occasionally it was my own thought). Over the years, the sheets have been distributed weekly by hand, by fax and by e-mail far and wide.

Now I am gratified to publish them in a book form, compiling five years of sheets. I thank my son Noach who has entered my handwritten material into a computer. Now, with G-d's help, I have learned to do that on my own.

My family has encouraged me to publish this book so that they and teachers and others will be able to use it to sharpen the understanding of children and adults at the Sabbath table and in schools. Above all, I owe gratitude to my dear wife Ethel who stands by my side to help me in every way she can.

With G-d's help, may I merit to publish another such book in five years' time.

1968 (5728)

BUILDING A SHUL
– AND A CONGREGATION

Not much later, the shul bought a property several miles farther out into suburban Baltimore, in an area called Randallstown, on Old Court Road, about a mile past where Yeshivas Chafetz Chaim, or Talmudical Academy – the day school where I had taught when I first arrived in Baltimore – had built a new campus. Plans were drawn up for a shul building, but it would be months before construction could begin. There was, however, an old house on the property, and so we turned it into a makeshift shul for the time being. It was a bit cramped, especially on holidays, but we arranged it into men's and ladies' sections, separated by a *mechitza*, as called for by Jewish law; and set up an ark where the Torahs were kept and a table on which the Torah was laid when it was read. What more did we need?

Over the course of that year and the next one, after the new shul building was erected and the old house demolished (we allowed the fire department to raze it as part of a training exercise for firefighter recruits) it wasn't always easy getting a *minyan*, or quorum of ten men needed to say certain prayers and publicly read the Torah, during the week. Morning services were early – around 6:30 a.m., so that those who attended could eat breakfast and get to work on time – and there were times when we found ourselves with the clock ticking the minutes away and only eight or nine men in the room.

I had an understanding, though, with some men in the neighborhood who would attend services only occasionally (like when they had a *yahrtzeit* – the anniversary of the death of a close relative – to observe by reciting the Kaddish prayer in memory of the deceased). Even if they could not be counted on to be in attendance every day, they would try to come. What was more – and this was the "clincher" – if we needed a "tenth man," they agreed to be on call for us to telephone them to help "make the *minyan*." And I never hesitated to make those phone calls when necessary. Even though I knew I was rousing them from their sleep, I also knew I was giving them a great opportunity, a Jewish spiritual merit.

I don't know what thoughts they might have had, or even expressed aloud, when, covers over their heads, they suddenly heard the phone ring and realized it was their lucky day. But I think they came in the end to think of their attendance those days as something to be proud of, at least once they were in shul and services could continue because of their presence.

I saw the shul as a holy trust, something it was an honor to care for. Not only "the shul" in the sense of the people who became members in its brotherhood and sisterhood, and attended services and celebrated life events there; but also "the shul" – the building itself.

Members who attended always helped out in every way, from setting out food for a Kiddush (a post-Sabbath services repast) to sweeping the floor to turning on the dozens of memorial plaque bulbs before a holiday when Yizkor, the special prayer on behalf of the deceased, would be recited.

But I always tried to take the lead, not only to set an example for others and not only to make them think of such work for a house of worship as an honor, but because it *was* an honor.

Michael is currently an observant Jewish husband and father. When he was a young boy, his family had belonged to the shul. He remembers being brought to shul as an eight-year-old, and seeing the rabbi studying with others before services. Michael says that the image of the rabbi's face as he studied Torah was the seed of his becoming fully observant years later.

During his teen-age years, Michael was a regular at shul. He recalls entering the shul building one day, at a time when no services were scheduled, to retrieve something he had left there. Noting lights on in the main sanctuary, he went to investigate.

Opening one of the doors to the large room, he saw a very tall freestanding ladder set up in an aisle among the seats. The room's ceiling was a good 25 feet high, and Michael's eyes

followed the rungs of the ladder up to its top, where one of a number of oversized chandeliers hung above. On a step near the ladder's top, with one hand grasping the ladder's side and the other one holding a light bulb, stood the rabbi.

Michael stood quietly, not wanted to startle him. But the rabbi, his ears attuned to every signal the shul might send, had heard the door open. Looking down at the unexpected visitor, he just smiled a hello.

"Rabbi Shafran," Michael said, "What in the world are you doing up there?"

The older man, wondering how the younger one could miss something so obvious, replied straightforwardly "Why, changing a bulb."

*"I know. But why are **you** doing it?"*

Again, a look of puzzlement crossed the rabbi's face.

"Because the old one burned out," he explained patiently.

Avi Shafran:

I was sixteen. We had moved to a middle-class, racially mixed, quiet suburban neighborhood. My father and I were walking to his synagogue, a few blocks from our new home. A young black boy, standing a few yards ahead of us, looked back in our direction and with an almost casual air of repugnance shouted "Heil Hitler!"

Most of my father's family perished at the hands of the Germans and their friends. He is not large in physical stature but has a deep pride in his Jewishness and a soul full of memories to match.

Before I could really digest the scene, my father had lurched from his spot and, with bounds that belied the limitations of his short legs, reached and grabbed the boy. The kid hadn't had the chance to run.

"Do you know what you said?" my father asked him.

"Heil Hitler," came the defiant reply, the boy apparently not satisfied with a simple answer in the affirmative.

I waited an endless few seconds, half expecting my father to deliver a forceful backhand slap to the sneering face. He didn't, though. He simply asked his prisoner where he lived. The boy pointed to a house across the street.

His grip tight on the boy's arm, my father walked up to the door at the front of the house and knocked; I followed close behind. A man half my father's age and twice his size answered. He seemed an average middle-class citizen, dressed in jeans and a tee-shirt, and the sounds from behind him testified to his having been watching television that Saturday afternoon when we interrupted his day. I felt strangely comforted by the man's seeming normalness, and imagined him reacting with deep disappointment, if not shock, at hearing the words his son had spat forth.

"That's my Poppa!" the boy exclaimed to us with defiance.

The father, not noticing at first that his son's arm was being held tightly in my own father's hand, addressed us without introduction.

"What do you want?"

"I would like you to please speak to your son about shouting rude things to passersby," my father answered.

"What did he say?"

My father told him.

"So what?" said Poppa, after only the slightest of pauses, "It's a

free country, man."

Then he noticed my father's grip on the youngster.

"And get your filthy hands off my boy!"

With that he pushed my father backwards with such force that he broke his grip on our prisoner.

My father's eyes seemed aflame.

"If you believe in such freedoms," he said loudly to the man, "then how would you like it if I shouted 'long live the KKK!'?"

The man's nostrils flared and he said, "You can say any ----- thing you like, Jew, but I might just tear you to shreds for it!"

With that reasoned explanation he shoved his considerable belly into my father's chest and raised his fist. My father knew he could never match the behemoth in a fight, not that he would fight even if he could have won, so he pushed the boy toward his Poppa and we turned and walked away.

In the meantime, a few other neighborhood boys had gathered, intrigued, no doubt, by the sight of the man in a suit and hat dragging one of their friends to his house. They had apparently overheard the exchange. As we walked by them we could hear them snicker and mumble things about Jews. From behind us, over and over, came calls of "Heil Hitler!"

After we had walked for a moment or two my father said, as much to himself as to me, "No matter where you go, you can't escape."

For the next year or so, before we moved to a different house about a mile away, it became a common occurrence to hear "Heil Hitler!" while walking to the synagogue, or even when driving through the neighborhood with the car windows open.

FRUITS OF THE SHUL

One of the things I am most proud of from our synagogue's years on Old Court Road was how so many young people who attended the shul then went on to become upstanding examples of how a Jewish life should be lived. During the 1970s the shul was host to an active chapter of the National Council of Synagogue Youth, or NCSY, which proved to be not only a good resource for young people already connected to the shul but a wonderful means, too, of involving young Jews in activities and events that took place there.

Among those activities were study sessions I held with groups of congregants. They were usually with small groups, on a Sabbath morning before services or, in the summer, on Sabbath afternoons. During the week, too, I studied various things – from Chumash, or Bible, to Talmud – with anyone interested in getting up early in the morning or willing to come to the shul at night.

One night, during a study session with several men in the shul's *beis medrash* – prayer and study room – the door suddenly burst open and two hooded men who seemed armed with weapons ordered us to empty our wallets, which of course we did. As soon as the intruders left, we called the police and they caught the pair – a sister of one of the culprits had apparently turned him in. One of the men in attendance at the study group and I testified at their trial and some of what was stolen was returned. From that day on, we kept the doors to the shul locked.

There was always a small group that came to shul before morning services each day – which began at 6:30 – to study Talmud with me. And there were other opportunities for studying with individuals, high school or college students, who wanted to learn Torah. I was privileged to conduct a weekly women's learning group as well for many years.

Some of the young people involved in the shul during those years became professionals of various types, but remained fully observant Jews. Others became Jewish educators themselves, teaching in yeshivas in the Baltimore area and beyond.

Although I was the main Torah-reader (having been one since my yeshiva days in Lithuania) and the main leader of services (the proper pronunciations and melodies were also things I picked up in Europe — much of it from Rabbi Krett in Salzheim), I always tried to involve the young men in particular in leading the services and reading the Torah. Many who were hesitant at first, once I pushed them a little harder to try (and was patient with the stumbles and falls), became accomplished service-leaders and Torah-readers. That fact, too, makes me very happy.

A Congregant:

My name isn't important but I was a regular at the shul during the 1970s and 1980s. By then, its name had become Adath Yeshurun-Mogen Abraham Congregation — reflecting a merger with another congregation that had become defunct. I remember how the rabbi not only delivered sermons each Shabbos and studied with groups of young and not-so-young people throughout the week, but also served as the shul's cantor and Torah-reader — at least when none of the young men he had taught the cantillation were prepared.

On Shabbos, services were generally held in the main sanctuary. During the week, a smaller study-hall sufficed for the ten to twenty men who attended morning services.

One weekday morning, though, services were held in the larger room — it may well have been some special occasion or holiday like Chanukah, or perhaps the heat was not working in the study-hall. Whatever the reason, the Torah from which the morning's reading was to be chanted was on the second tier of the ark where the Torahs were kept.

The ark was a large and beautiful repository for the scrolls, with doors shaped like the popular conception of the Tablets of the Law that Moses brought down from Mt. Sinai. The doors slid open to each side, revealing a sheer blue curtain behind which the Torahs stood upright. The ones in current use were usually

placed on the lower of the two tiers; the Torahs that had been rolled to other readings were generally put on the upper level.

The rabbi is not a tall man, but he is an energetic, determined and physically strong one. So when a Torah on the upper shelf needed to be brought down for use, the younger people in the congregation usually deferred to him. Even the heavier Torahs didn't seem hard for him to handle.

That morning was no different. He took hold of the atzei chaim, *the wooden poles around which the Torah's parchment was wrapped — whose bottoms protruded beneath the body of the Torah and served as handles for lifting it — and slowly brought the Torah down toward him.*

I don't know exactly what happened next. Whether the heavy silver crown — a large ornament placed atop the Torah on Sabbaths and holidays — had been on the Torah itself and somehow worked its way loose from its moorings (the tops of the atzei chaim, onto which the crown's specially constructed bottom fit), or had been sitting on the shelf and was snagged by the Torah's cloth; what I do know is that it toppled down and hit the rabbi square on his face. He held tight to the Torah but the crown had opened a good-sized gash on his lip, which was bleeding quite heavily.

One congregant rushed to pick up the fallen crown and several others ran over to the rabbi but he waved them away. He

whipped out a handkerchief, which he held against his lip, and continued the service.

Everyone watched in amazement as he ascended the bima, *the platform holding a large table on which the Torah was laid and opened for reading. He opened the scroll, announced the first man honored with saying the blessings over the Torah and proceeded as on any other Torah-reading morning, chanting the verses as if nothing untoward had happened. As he read, he held the now-crimson handkerchief away from his mouth, and his lip welled with new blood. When he completed each portion, he applied pressure to the wound to stanch the bleeding. After services, he assured those present that he would seek whatever medical care was needed.*

Rochel (Shafran) Zoberman:

The very first time I ever attended Shabbos services in a shul other than my father's I was taken aback. The rabbi delivered a sermon but someone else read from the Torah, and other people conducted the actual services. I had always assumed that it was the norm for the rabbi of a shul to do all that — and blow the shofar on Rosh Hashana and tend to the shul's physical needs and make sure that it was clean...

PART OF ME GONE

The most terrible day of my life came without warning. My wife had undergone heart surgery several years earlier, but she had seemed, if slowly so, on the road to full recovery. I would help her get the exercise her doctor had prescribed by walking with her several times around the quiet court on which our house was located, and she took her medicines as prescribed.

On my way home from my city auditor's job one evening, I made a stop at a furniture store, where I picked up some new chairs my wife and I had earlier chosen and bought for our kitchen table. When I arrived home, I found her collapsed at that very table. She had suffered a stroke and did not respond to me. I immediately called 911 and she was rushed to the hospital.

Over the next days, although she was breathing on her own, she showed no signs of consciousness. My children all quickly came – my daughter Rochel from Toronto, Canada, my son Avi from Providence, Rhode Island and my son Noach who lived locally, in the Ner Israel yeshiva campus faculty housing – to stand vigil with me at their mother's bedside. We spoke to her and looked for any sign of response to our words and touches. We occasionally thought we sensed some, but there were no clear indications of awareness.

When, in the middle of the night several days later, she was called by her Creator, I was a broken man. My Paitche was gone, and she had become my life. I felt as if there was no way to move forward in time.

Even though the funeral took place only hours after she left the world, it was attended by a large crowd. She had served the shul for almost 40 years, and had served, too, as a president of the Ladies' Auxiliary of the Ner Israel yeshiva.

More, though; she had touched — and changed — so many lives, not only those of our shul's congregants but anyone she met. But, of course, all the love and mourning that poured out from Baltimore's community couldn't approach my own.

Eulogies were delivered by Ner Israel's Rosh Yeshiva, or dean, Rabbi Yaakov Weinberg, may his memory be a blessing; and by myself and my sons. We laid my wife to rest in a cemetery outside of the city where her mother — who had passed on ten years earlier — father, brother and grandmother lay. It was also the resting place of the renowned founder and Rosh Yeshiva of the Ner Israel yeshiva, Rabbi Yitzchok Yaakov Ruderman, and his wife; and would later become the resting place for my wife's surviving brother Moshe and his wife Betty, and for Rabbi Ruderman's son-in-law and successor, Rabbi Weinberg (whose wife, may she be well, was one of my wife's closest friends) — may the memory of them all be a blessing.

Avi Shafran:

We felt so helpless, we siblings, watching our father founder in the wake of our mother's death. The week-long shiva mourning period had been cathartic, as shivas are. But even the wonderful things we hadn't known about our mother but heard about from visitors over the course of that week couldn't really comfort us. And our father was even more distraught. We worried about him, how he would manage on his own, how bereft of hope he seemed.

I remember thinking about how we take the very will to live, the ability to persevere, for granted, but shouldn't. A verse from Tehillim we recite three times a day suddenly took on new meaning. I had always wondered about it — it is, the Talmud says, the central verse in the Ashrei prayer — since its grammar seems puzzling. "You open your hands," it addressed G-d, "and satiate all living things, will [ratzon]" — the latter word's placement and intention far from clear. According to Your will? Willful living things? "Will," meaning what living things need?

What occurred to me was that "will" might be read simply, as the object of the satiation. G-d satiates all living things with will itself. He provides us not only our physical sustenance but our emotional sustenance no less. He gives us the will, when we feel despair, to go on.

Pesach was only weeks away, and our father insisted that the three of us and our families spend the holiday with him in the house. Not only could we not think of saying no, we cherished the opportunity to celebrate a Jewish holiday together as a multi-branched family, even if someone so very essential to who we were would not be present. In a way, we felt she was.

It was a bittersweet holiday, certainly, but festive all the same, and it was hard for the two of us who lived far away — I in Providence, Rhode Island, and my sister in Toronto — to say goodbye to our father. We worried about him, and prayed that he find and recognize future blessings in his life.

Our prayers were answered. His life until then had been a lesson in resilience, and he quickly undertook all that was needed to care for himself, expanding his cooking skills and maintaining the house, even as he continued to work as an auditor for the city and — above all else — to fulfill his role as the rabbi of a congregation.

February, 1990 (Shevat, 5749)

AFTER LOSS, BLESSING

The mother of my children was gone, although she lived on in those children and in theirs. One of our grandchildren and two of our grandchildren's own children, not to mention the daughters of some congregants and friends of my late wife – even received her name, Puah.

Over the months after I became a widower, whenever I was approached and asked if I was interested in meeting someone special, I was very hesitant.

One day, though, Rabbi Yaakov Kulefsky, may his memory be a blessing, who at the time was one of the main lecturers at Ner Israel (and would eventually serve as the yeshiva's Rosh Yeshiva for a short while) called me on the phone and asked me to come to his apartment at the yeshiva to speak with him. He wouldn't disclose what he wanted to speak about, but out of respect for the great scholar he was, I paid the visit.

What he wanted was to ask me to meet a woman, a widow living in New York whom he knew from her visits to her daughter and son-in-law – Rabbi Simcha Cook, a rebbe, like my son Noach, in the Ner Israel high school program. As it happened, my wife had known Mrs. Cook and had been very fond of her.

At first, I said no, thank you. I didn't feel ready to meet anyone as a marriage prospect. But Rabbi Kulefsky would not let me go so easily and so I promised him I would think about it, which I did. Several days later, I called him to tell him I would be happy to meet Mrs. Ethel Bagry, and within several weeks we became engaged.

Our marriage ceremony took place in the shul's social hall, with Rabbi Weinberg presiding and Rabbi Kulefsky, our "matchmaker," among the other prominent local rabbis present.

Avi Shafran:

Our father was introduced to a wonderful woman — how many have marveled at the good fortune he had in marriage — who became our stepmother. She was a widow by the name of Ethel Bagry (born Mendlowitz, in Scranton, Pennsylvania), and when our father brought her to visit my wife and our family in Providence, we were captivated by her kindness, good cheer and youth. Actually, "Bobby Ethel"— the Bobby was a form of the Yiddish word for "grandmother"— had been born before our

father was, but she exuded an inner youthfulness that impressed everyone who came to meet her.

No one, of course, could ever replace our mother, but I felt that Bobby Ethel became a "second mother" to us, and a loving grandmother to our children, and to all her new husband's grandchildren.

Shlomo, a young member of the shul and regular at some of the rabbi's classes, wanted to propose marriage to the young woman he had been seeing. Katie was a professional Russian translator and Shlomo, who knew not a word of Russian, decided he wanted to propose in that language. He hoped that the young lady might be impressed, or amused, enough by his having taken the time to prepare his proposal, to actually say yes.

As he did with so many things, he turned to his rabbi for help. Might he know the right Russian words? Although Rabbi Shafran did know a number of Russian phrases from his sojourn in Siberia during the Second World War, he did not want to take a chance with something so potentially important. So he begged off for the moment but soon thereafter, while driving, saw someone he realized had been study-ing Russian in college. Motioning to the student to stop, the rabbi asked him how to

say "Will you marry me?" in Russian. The student may have been puzzled momen-tarily but Rabbi Shafran explained the situation, and received the appropriate words, which he duly delivered to Shlomo.

Even though Shlomo ended up (as his wife later informed him) stating "You will be my wife" rather than making the request he had intended, he was successful in getting the answer he had hoped for. The couple has been married now for nearly 25 years and have several children.

1989 (5729)

A SPECIAL SHUL FAMILY

There were many individuals and families in the neighborhood who came to be deeply involved in the shul. One such family that, almost from the opening of the shul at its Randallstown location, became particularly close to both my wife and me – and later with my second wife – were the Gerstmans.

It was 1969 when Sol and Gail Gerstman and their three little boys moved to a house near Talmudical Academy, or "TA." Mrs. Gerstman had been raised in a Sabbath-observant home. Mr. Gerstman was raised in a family that wasn't religiously observant but had belonged to a "traditional" synagogue. During his service in the U.S. army, his mother died and he encountered Jewish religious observance on a personal level for the first time. A group of Jewish men serving with him made sure to gather a *minyan* so that he could recite Kaddish.

By the time the Gerstmans moved to Baltimore, they were an observant Jewish family, and had to choose between the two local congregations: one that met at "TA" and our shul. Their first Shabbos in the neighborhood they attended the shul, and never left.

My first wife and I were very happy to welcome the Gerstmans, who we soon came to feel were very much a part of the congregational family – and of our own family in a way. They became not only dear friends but mainstays of the shul, tireless workers on its behalf. In time, Sol became very active in the shul and served for many years as *gabbai*, or "ritual director." In that role, he made sure that services ran smoothly and that synagogue ritual honors were bestowed properly and fairly. He served as well as vice president and then as president of the congregation; and Gail became a trusted confidante of my wife's and an indispensable member of the shul's Ladies' Auxiliary.

Sol Gerstman:

My wife and I and our boys were invited to the Shafrans' Pesach Seder shortly after our arrival in the neighborhood. Our two older sons, then 10 and 8 years of age, peppered the rabbi with questions. He would offer an answer and then retrieve one or another Hebrew book to show them its basis. The rabbi would never put off a question until later. If it was important enough for a child to ask, it was important enough to do his best to answer. And he always went to the books, saying that seeing something "inside" was invaluable. "Osyos machkimos" —

"Letters make one wise"— he would say. That attention to words and their meanings would, over coming years and with the rabbi's determined teaching and encourage-ment, help our sons become accomplished congregational Torah-readers.

We remember, too, how strong a supporter Rabbi Shafran was of having the shul put resources into a youth group, the NCSY chapter it came to host in the 1970s. At board meetings, some members questioned "what good it would do" to expend the shul's limited capital on an NCSY charter and the costs associated with the various youth activities and Shabbatonim — weekend retreats for guests — that the undertak-ing would entail.

But the rabbi was insistent on having the chapter established and funded. He under-stood, as we and some others at the time did, that the youth of the shul, along with all Jewish youth, were, simply put, the Jewish future.

The chapter was formed and the years that followed yielded many "dividends" on the investment. Whenever we visit Park Heights, the Jewish neighborhood where many of the shul's young people moved after they had married and established families, we see those dividends in beautiful observant Jewish families whose roots go back to the shul's NCSY.

Years later, in 1985, I was in the hospital with a back ailment. On the day of my mother's yahrtzeit *[death anniversary], Rabbi*

Shafran showed up in my hospital room with eight other Jewish men in tow, so that we could hold services with a minyan, or quorum, and I could recite Kaddish in my mother's memory.

And when, in 2006, I underwent back surgery and was recuperating in my home, Rabbi Shafran made sure to visit on my father's yahrtzeit to study Mishneh with me in my father's merit.

Gail Gerstman:

Snow had blanketed Baltimore the previous night. My husband Sol had managed to get his car out of the driveway — he had gone to services at the shul early that morning as usual — so I didn't expect to have trouble getting to work myself.

But it had snowed more since Sol had left for shul and so, as I backed my own car out, the car's wheels began spinning and I saw that I wasn't going anywhere very quickly.

Realizing that Sol was planning to go straight to work from shul, I quickly ran into the house and called the shul to try to catch him and have him make a detour home first to dig me out of the icy rut.

Rabbi Shafran answered the phone and when I asked to speak to my husband, the rabbi told me that services had ended and that Sol had already left for work.

I must have sounded distressed — well, I was — because the rabbi asked me why I needed Sol.

I told him but explained that I had to hang up, since I would have to walk the several blocks to Talmudical Academy, the school where I worked. I prepared myself for the walk and headed for the front door.

Through the window I saw Rabbi Shafran. He had driven to the house to free my car from the ice, which he proceeded to do.

Eric Horowitz:

I began studying Talmud with Rabbi Shafran regularly in the 1980s and have continued ever since. Even after my family and I moved away from the shul neighborhood so that our children would be near their friends and have a larger Jewish community around them, we have continued our study-sessions.

For years, in fact, I happily walked several miles on Shabbos, from Park Heights to Randallstown, just for the privilege. In

more recent years, when Rabbi Shafran would spend an occasional Shabbos at his son Noach and daughter-in-law Shalva's apartment on the Ner Israel yeshiva campus, he would walk several miles in one direction and I would do the same in the other direction so that we could meet at Talmudical Academy to keep up our Sabbath afternoon study session.

I find it interesting that although Rashi [the premier commentary on the Torah and Talmud] graces every page of Tanach [the Torah, Prophets and Writings] and the Talmud, we know relatively little about his life. His greatest contribution to the world was his insight in Torah. Not much else matters.

As I look back over the past 20 years with Rabbi Shafran, I feel something similar. We spent much time together, but it was almost all dedicated to Torah study. I associate his face with a page of Talmud.

And his dedication was tremendous. Many times he trudged through feet of snow early in the morning or late at night so that he wouldn't miss a class or study-session. Several times we studied by candlelight when the electricity was interrupted by a storm. Even if one of us wasn't feeling well, we made the effort to keep our commitment to our study.

One funny thing sticks in my mind: so many times when Rabbi Shafran would fetch a tome to check a source pertinent to something we were studying, he seemed to somehow open it immediately to the right page. It was, and is, quite uncanny.

Avi Shafran:

So many things are so different when regarded through Jewish eyes. Even what a New Year's day means. To the wider world, January 1 is a day of partying and revelry, an opportunity to get drunk and have a good time. Rosh Hashana, by contrast, is a time of judgment — a time of happiness, to be sure, but of trepidation as well, of regret, of apologies, of repentance.

My father always blew the shofar himself at his shul on Rosh Hashana. And, in fact, many years he would blow it as well (another hundred blasts — and even one is not easy) for the residents of a nursing home — and, once again (the full complement), for a quadriplegic in the neighborhood where he lived.

The blasts of the ram's horn call all who hear them, in Maimonides' words, to "awaken, sleepers, from your slumber," to reject the "silly distractions of the temporal world" we occupy; to focus on what alone is real: serving our Creator and being good to one another. To see the world, in other words, through Jewish eyes. No wonder my father was so happy to discover that the comfortable Yom Kippur shoes he had found (leather footwear is forbidden on the fast) were "shofar shoes."

I didn't understand at first what a "shofar shoe" was, though, and told him. He smiled and responded patiently, "Well, each one has a shofar on it."

When I expressed skepticism, he went to his bedroom and emerged triumphantly with the footwear.

And when he held them up for me to see, his Jewish eyes taught mine a lesson.

I'll never look at the Nike "swoosh" quite the same way again.

Excerpted from "His Way Is The Torah," by Adam Stone,
Baltimore Jewish Times, January 25, 2002,
*(published as Congregation Adath Yeshurun-Mogen Abraham
commemorated Rabbi Simcha Shafran's fiftieth year
as its spiritual leader)*

What a wonderful world it would be if everyone were as nice as Rabbi Simcha Shafran. Rabbi Shafran, spiritual leader of Adath Yeshurun-Mogen Abraham Congregation in Randallstown, has lasted 50 years in the same job — a virtual miracle by rabbinic standards.

Ask him how, and he'll tell you sincerely that the key lies in "understanding" and "cooperation," in achieving a "rapport" with the congregation.

Call it the "Rabbi Shafran Paradox." On the one hand, all this tender talk is true: The man has a reputation as being one of the warmest, funniest, most approachable rabbis in town. At the same time, he is proud to remain the reigning champion of Baltimore's religious hard-liners.

"We have so much freedom in the United States, and that is a good thing, of course," he said. "At the same time, it lends itself to people who may abuse this freedom and perhaps — though they mean to improve religion — they may in fact be destroying it. Freedom can be a good thing, and it can also be detrimental. Too much freedom is anarchy."

While he may fear too much freedom in religious life, Rabbi Shafran has seen the brutality that comes with too little freedom. Born in 1925, he grew up in a small town in Poland and lost most of his family to the Nazi horrors...

From those experiences, he took away "the need for unity among the Jewish people, the knowledge that there is one nation, one G-d, and that we have to feel that sense of responsibility to one another, to do whatever we can to help one another," he said. "That is what I was taught in yeshiva, and that was the life in Europe that I saw."

To that end, the rabbi has been active in the wider community throughout his many years with the synagogue. For years he has acted as a lead player in the city's bais din, or religious court. He also championed the effort to designate in Randallstown an eruv, or Shabbat ritual enclosure...

"He has been extremely helpful, a blessing to the Randallstown community, holding it together for many years," said Rabbi Sholom Salfer, spiritual leader of the Winands Road Synagogue Center in Randallstown.

Moreover, Rabbi Shafran's unswerving devotion to Halacha, or Jewish law, has set the tone for his rabbinical colleagues and for the community as a whole.

"It gives us an anchor," said Rabbi Salfer. "If he can put his foot down, then I can put my foot down too. He is not rigid,

but he is uncompromising where it would be disastrous to compromise. He has principles. He is a courageous person.

Courageous, yes, but first and foremost: A person.

"His way is the Torah and that is his only way of thinking, but he is also very sweet, very warm," said Alan Friedenberg, 39, whose family has attended Adath Yeshurun for more than 40 years. "I have always known that I could go to him with any kind of questions, whether it be something halachic, or something personal, or something I had trouble understanding on a philosophical level."

As with most synagogues, Adath Yeshurun has had its ups and downs over the years. . . The congregation eventually migrated to Pimlico Road and, in 1968 moved to its present location in the outermost reaches of Pikesville, almost in Randallstown.

At the time of the move, the synagogue had about 50 members. In subsequent years that number grew to a high of 120, but has declined to about 50 congregants again.

Rabbi Shafran is perfectly ready to acknowledge that his strict interpretations of Jewish law may have driven some of that decline.

"When we built this shul, there were some members who wanted to build it in such a way that would be objectionable

according to Halacha, for example by having a microphone during services," he recalled. "I said no, I would not allow it, and the person who wanted that said they would no longer be a member. I said that that was fine."

Such instances are the rare exception, however, in a congregation that has by and large stood by its rabbi as he has endeavored to safeguard the letter of the law.

The freedom and openness of American society today make it easier than ever for Jews to opt out of a life imbued with — or as some say, constrained by — strict ritual observance. Yet Rabbi Shafran is certain his worldview will endure long after he is gone. "I am absolutely optimistic, no question," he said.

"In the 1950s and 1960s, I knew every Orthodox Jew in Baltimore. Now I could not possibly know everybody, because the numbers have increased so tremendously. So why should I not be optimistic?" he said. . .

AN ERA ENDS

During the 1980s and 1990s, many congregants – including some who had grown up in the shul, married and started families – began moving away. They didn't want to leave the neighborhood, but almost all of their children's friends, and many of their own, lived in the Park Heights and Greenspring communities, miles away. And so, with some reluctance but understandably, they relocated. As a result, much of the energy that powered the shul was lost.

During those years, I worked hard, along with others, to oversee the building of an *eruv* – a ritual enclosure made of wire or string that enables observant Jews to carry items outside of their homes on Shabbos – to encompass the Pikesville-Randallstown area that included the shul and surrounding neighborhoods. My hope was that if young mothers in the area were able – like those in the more established and successful Park Heights and Greenspring areas – to wheel baby strollers and carriages on the Sabbath, perhaps the neighborhood might attract more observant families.

The *eruv* was, in fact built, but the return, unfortunately, was not realized. Maybe we started the project too late. It was disappointing, of course, but I always try to see the positive. And here there was a great positive: the many non-observant Jews within the enclosure, who – whether or not they cared, or even knew it – had been violating the Sabbath every time they carried something outside on Shabbos were now no longer doing so.

Despite the changes in the neighborhood, until around 2000 the shul persevered, with classes and services daily, including Shabbos and holidays.

What had become apparent, though, was that there were simply not enough observant Jews in the neighborhood to justify the shul's continuation. And so, after consulting with the members of the board and those who regularly attended services, a decision was reached to close the shul and sell the property.

Letter to the editor, *Baltimore Jewish Times,*
May 23, 2008

Editor:

Recently, our synagogue, Adath Yeshurun Congregation, closed its doors ("Shul to Close," BJT, December 14, 2007). It was by all accounts a poor synagogue, but I found it a place of deeply religious fervor and all because of the rabbi...

Rabbi Simcha Shafran gave so much to all who entered. He led Talmud classes with all who would partake. He was always there, leading us, showing us, giving us his everything. He was so kind and cared for even a tiny ant, which, when [one appeared] in our shul, he would gently let crawl on a piece of paper and then let it go on its way outside.

He is not famous, but the world would be much better were there more great rabbis like our Rabbi Simcha Shafran.

Irving Distenfeld

Baltimore

2008 (5769)

A NEW STAGE OF LIFE

Thirty years earlier, it had been very painful for me to see the previous shul building, which had been sold to a fraternal lodge, quickly "turned around" and resold to a church group. While Judaism has respect for other faiths that believe in one G-d, a Jewish house of worship is not permitted to be used for a Christian house of worship. This time, I was not going to take any chances. I insisted that the contract of sale stipulate that the shul building would be razed and that, as per the declared intention of a buyer we had found, residences would be erected on the land. The buyer accepted those conditions and signed the contract.

With the deal struck, at the High Holiday services of the Jewish year 5768 (2007) I announced to the small congregation – once it had numbered in the hundreds on those special days of the year but now there were no more than 20 people present – that that Rosh Hashana and Yom Kippur would be the last ones to be marked in that edifice. It was a sad moment for me, and I think for the others too.

There were two things, though – well, three, if I included my own future – that had to be taken care of. First there was the shul's name, which I felt a responsibility to perpetuate, to memorialize not only the shul's history and accomplishments but the hard work of so many in its behalf over the years. And, second, the memorial plaques marking the names and birth and death dates of deceased members or living members' deceased relatives that hung in the shul's lobby and study hall had to have a new home. Over the years, members of the shul had underwritten those plaques – some of which recalled the lives of people who lived in the 1800s – with their donations. I felt a responsibility to make sure that the memorial tablets would, in some holy Jewish place in Baltimore, continue to reflect the memory of the names and lives of those recorded on them.

Then there were other things to address, like what to do with the shul's religious items, its Torahs, holy books, prayer books and other things.

In the end, I decided – with the shul board's consent – that the shul should offer proceeds of the sale of its property to an existing shul that I felt reflected its ideals, a shul that would consent to perpetuating our shul's name and to providing a place for its memorial tablets. A perfect fit, I decided, would be the Agudath Israel of Greenspring congregation. Its rabbi, Rabbi Mordechai Shuchatowitz, was, and is, a respected scholar and the *dayan kavua*, or main judge, on the Baltimore community's Bais Din, or religious court, which I was privileged to serve as its *mazkir*, or administrator. And so I approached Rabbi Shuchatowitz and the officers of his shul with the idea, and they were receptive. Agudath Israel of Greenspring-Adath Yeshurun/Mogen Abraham Congregation was born. A long name, perhaps, but it has to hold a lot of history.

Another local shul, Shomrei Emunah, had expressed interest in part of our shul building's façade, twelve hewn marble columns adorned with beautiful carvings of the symbols of the Twelve Tribes of Israel. Back when the shul building was being erected, one of the members whose business had him travel to Italy obtained the special marble on one of his trips and donated it to the shul. I worked with him and the architect on the design. What resulted was indeed very impressive, and I was happy that, in addition to the Torahs and other holy items, the columns, too, would have a new home.

Which left only the question of what I would be doing once the shul was taken down. It was clear that my wife and I would be moving from the neighborhood. There were only a handful of people in the area connected to the shul left, and most of them were also planning on relocating. I have been blessed with generally good health, thank G-d, and had no desire to "retire" from what I have spent the past 56 years doing.

And so I spent about a year looking at homes in various other neighborhoods where I felt I might be able to offer something of worth, ideally in the form of a *minyan* and *beis medrash* – a place to pray and to study. What I finally decided on was a house in what Baltimoreans call the "Smith Avenue" area – with a large finished basement that could be transformed into a shul/study hall. With the help of some shul members, I had moved the small ark from the *beis medrash* of the shul, and the Torah-reading table, to our house. Now we moved them again to our new home — home and *beis medrash*, that is.

There are several synagogues in the vicinity, but my main interest was in hosting Shabbos morning services, and I didn't see my plans as interfering with any of the established congregations. As it happened, several members of the shul who had moved away live nearby, and some of them were happy to rejoin me in my new abode. In particular, Chaim and Laura Leventhal, and Arnold Cummins, have been truly helpful in helping us settle in to our new home and in helping me set up the *beis medrash* in our basement.

A Friday night "house-*minyan*" already existed in a home on the same block, so, rather than interfere with it, I set my sights on only a Shabbos morning *minyan*. So far, it has functioned fairly smoothly, although I hope that in future months it will attract enough "regulars" for me not to have to make calls to ensure that we'll have the necessary quorum. My basement *beis medrash* also serves as a place for studying with others and holding *shiurim*, or study-classes in the evening.

Although I am kept busy with my work on behalf of the Baltimore Bais Din, my wife and I also do a good amount of travelling. We don't go on vacations. Neither of us has any desire to see the world or to relax anywhere but at home. What we enjoy is participating in the happy occasions of our children — my wife considers mine to be hers, and I feel that hers are mine — and in those of our respective grandchildren. And — how unthinkable it once was but which Divine mercy has granted — those of our great-grandchildren. And so we are still happy to drive to Lakewood, New Jersey or to New York to be part of such celebrations.

January, 2008 (Shevat, 5768)

Avi Shafran:

Paying a "shiva call," visiting a neighbor who had lost a close relative, I noticed a man, another visitor, looking at me repeatedly. After speaking with the mourners, I moved my chair back to the back of the group of visitors present, to allow others to have closer access to those in mourning. I found myself seated near the man who had been looking at me.

"Excuse me," he said, "I think I was at your daughter's wedding a few months ago."

One of our daughters had in fact been married earlier that year and the gentleman knew the groom's parents, which was why he had been present. And, as it happened, he worked for my neighbor, the man sitting shiva. I was surprised that he had recognized me and had remembered from where.

"Well," he said, "I remember the wedding well; I had a great time there. I even have a picture I took of the most amazing thing there."

And with that he took out his phone, one of those equipped with a built-in camera, punched around on the thing for a few

seconds and then smiled broadly when he found what he was looking for.

"Here it is! I was so impressed with him, I kept the photo on my phone!"

"Impressed with whom?" I asked.

"With the distinguished older man — I heard he was a relative of the bride — who was so lively, who danced so energetically! Look at him! He's kicking up a storm like a youngster!"

I looked at the screen. It was tiny, but there could be no mistaking what it showed.

"That's my father," I informed he man with a smile, "may he be well."

Chaim Leventhal:

We had been privileged to live next door to the Shafrans for several years in the "Old Court Road" neighborhood before my family and I moved to our current home. When things worked out for the Rabbi and Rebbetzin to move to our new neighborhood, we were very happy. It has been a privilege to know and study with and learn from Rabbi Shafran for all these years, and it has been a privilege for me to be able to help him with various maintenance and repairs in his new home and beis medrash.

Shortly after we moved into our previous home, I volunteered to show the rabbi — who still happily mows his lawn himself — how to operate a gas-powered "weed-whacker." What happened during that demonstration — which went a little awry — is something that I think captures well who the rabbi is.

As I revved up the machine's motor one of the tzitzis — the tassels attached to the tallis koton, the four-cornered undershirt worn by observant Jewish men — somehow got sucked into the rotor, which tore it to shreds.

Without the slightest hesitation, the rabbi reached over and pulled off the tallis koton. He had realized, before I had, that wearing a four-cornered garment without tzitzis — special fringes — on each corner is a violation of Jewish law.

On another occasion, one Shabbos, I pointed out to the rabbi how a beautiful rainbow had appeared in the sky. What he saw when he looked out the window, though, was no mere rainbow. It was an opportunity for a bracha, a blessing — the one traditionally made on such an occasion.

That constant awareness of a Jew's obligations has made a great impression on me and my family, and continues to do so.

Noach Shafran:

A number of years ago, the administration of the Ner Israel Yeshiva's "Mechina," or high school division — where I am privileged to serve as an 11th grade rebbe, or religious studies teacher — asked me if I would undertake to teach a history class as well, on the Holocaust, as part of the secular studies curriculum.

The teaching of the Holocaust in yeshivos —especially with the inclusion of elements of the Shoah that are, unfortunately, inadequately covered by conventional historical treatments — had long been made an urgent priority by many contemporary yeshiva deans and by Torah Umesorah, the Orthodox Jewish umbrella group that services yeshivas and day schools across North America.

I hesitated at first, having no formal training in history. But after much encouragement from the administration, and after spending a good amount of time educating myself about the topic, I accepted the additional position and have been teaching the class for nearly a decade. It has been a wonderful experience for me personally, as I have become much more knowledgeable about the Jewish European world and its terrible destruction; and I think the hundreds of students who have taken the course with me recognize that they have benefitted greatly as well.

In 2005, I was able to be part of a trip to Eastern Europe, partially underwritten by a Holocaust commemoration group and designed to give teachers of Holocaust studies a greater familiarity with the cities, communities and edifices that figure into what they teach.

A regular part of my course is asking my father to address my students. I have occasionally had other survivors of the war years present their personal accounts but each year I invite him — as other schools have done as well. He always accepts and tells of his own childhood in Poland, his experiences in yeshiva, his banishment to Siberia and his subsequent yeshiva study in Germany.

The students — there can be up to 50 in each class — are always rapt, seized by his presentation. They often ask him questions, which sometimes jog his memory and elicit interesting facts.

More than once, he has called the students' attention to his shoes, which are a small size but unusually wide. "Why do you think I wear a size 6 1/2 EEE ?" he asks. Of course no one has any idea what he is getting at.

Then he explains with a smile. "As a child I didn't usually have shoes that were bought for me. I wore whatever shoes my older brother had outgrown. They were usually too small for me too but I was next in line for them so I wore them. I think the development of the bones in my feet was stunted by the hand-me-downs and, confined to too-small shoes, my feet grew wider rather than longer."

I think his words about that minor matter have probably brought more than a few of his American listeners to think about their closets.

When he speaks to the class, especially when talking about his family, he often shows great emotion, sometimes having to pause and collect himself before continuing.

Once I asked him if he enjoys speaking to the classes. His answer, though he didn't use the word, was no. He told me that he relives what he recounts, and that it is very painful to remember his childhood years and the events that came to pass.

I asked him if he would rather not talk to the classes. He said simply: "I have to. It needs to be done."

EPILOGUE

September, 2006 (Elul, 5766)

D ovie's parents, like most Jewish ones, were somewhat protective, and apprehensive about putting the 14-year-old on a train to travel alone from the New York area to Baltimore, where he attended the high school division of the yeshiva known as Ner Israel Rabbinical College. He had arranged to get a ride back to yeshiva after the Sukkos holiday with a postgraduate student but the ride had evaporated, so Dovie's mother and father had no choice.

To save their son a cab ride from the downtown Baltimore train station, they asked Dovie's paternal grandfather, a respected Baltimore rabbi, if he might be able to pick the boy up at the station and take him to the yeshiva.

"Of course!" he replied, as they knew he would. He and his wife, Dovie's step-grandmother, would do anything for any of their grandchildren. To take his grandson to yeshiva was a special pleasure for him.

The next day, Dovie's mother took him to a train station in New Jersey. After seeing him board the train, she received a call on her cellphone from her husband, at work in Manhattan.

"Did you make it on time?" he asked. "Yes," she reassured him. "He's on the train and it's about to depart."

Dovie's father went back to work, and his mother returned home.

Their son's trip was uneventful. His train arrived a bit later than expected but Dovie's grandfather was there waiting patiently, and shuttled him to yeshiva.

In the car, the two conversed, about the holiday just past, about how the boy was doing in yeshiva. And then, as they approached their destination, the grandfather asked his grandson if the train ride he had taken had been his first.

"Yes," answered Dovie.

"There isn't time now," said the grandfather, Rabbi Simcha Shafran, "but one day, remind me to tell you about my own first train trip.

"I was just about your age."

GLOSSARY OF HEBREW, YIDDISH
AND ARAMAIC WORDS

Alter – "elder"

arba minim – the "four species" of plants/fruit waved on the holiday of Sukkos

atzei chaim – the two wooden dowels around which a Torah scroll is rolled, which extend above the parchment of the scroll

bar-mitzvah – a Jewish boy come of age (13) regarding his obligation to observe Jewish law; informally: the celebration of that milestone

beis din – a Jewish court

beis medrash – room or hall dedicated to prayer and study

bima – the platform in a synagogue sanctuary supporting a large table on which the Torah is laid and opened when read publicly

bitochon – trust in G-d's knowing what is best

challa – braided Sabbath bread

cheder – Jewish studies school for young boys

cholent – special stew traditionally eaten at the Sabbath day-meal

davening – prayer or praying

dayan kavua – a "set" or main judge in a Jewish court

Eliyahu – Elijah the Prophet, according to Jewish tradition, the harbinger of the messianic age

Eruv – an "enclosure," generally made of poles and wires or string, bounding off an area within which Jews will be permitted to carry items outdoors on the Sabbath

gabbai – ritual director in a synagogue

galach – Christian priest

Haftarah – synagogue reading from the Prophets, following the Torah reading

halacha – Jewish religious law (adjective: halachic)

hashgacha pratis – G-d's focus on and guidance of each individual

Hashomer Hatzair – secular, socialist Israeli kibbutz movement

Kaddish – special prayer of praise recited, among other times, on the anniversary of the death of a close relative

kibbutz – Israeli collective farm

kiruv – the "bringing close" of non-observant or minimally observant Jews to the fullness of the Jewish religious tradition

kumsizt – Yiddish for "come and sit"; a serene and earnest yet festive gathering of song and stories

machzor – special prayer book for holidays

mamzer – progeny of certain marriages forbidden by Jewish law, (plural: mamzerim)

matzos – unleavened bread eaten on Passover

Mazkir – administrator of a Jewish court

mechitza – "separation"-barrier between men's and women's sections in synagogue

melamed – teacher of Torah to young boys

mikveh – Jewish ritual bath

minyan – quorum of Jewish men required for certain prayers

mishloach manos – gifts of food traditionally sent to friends on the holiday of Purim

Mishneh – the holy text that forms the backbone of the Talmud, the record of Judaism's "Oral Law"

mitzvah – literally "commandment"; fulfillment of a requirement or practice of good deed

Moshiach – the Messiah

mussar – literally: "tradition"; the study of ethical texts and their application to life

nafcha – blacksmith

nussach – style of prayer

Oneg Shabbos – "enjoyment of the Sabbath"; informally: a celebratory gathering or repast on, and in honor of, the Sabbath

parsha – weekly Torah-reading portion

Pinchas – the name of a biblical figure and the Torah-portion that begins with his appointment as a cohein, or priestly caste member

poritz – powerful landowner in pre-war Eastern Europe

Rashi – Rabbi Shlomo Yitzchaki, the premier medieval commentary on the Torah and Talmud

Shabbos – the Jewish Sabbath

Shabbos Braishis – the first Sabbath after Simchas Torah, when the synagogue public reading of the Torah is begun anew

Shalom Aleichem – greeting, and welcoming song traditionally sung at the start of

Shavuos – the early summer festival on which the giving of the Torah at Mt. Sinai is celebrated

Shehecheyanu – a special blessing recited when an occasion, observance or fruit is experienced for the first time that year

Shemini Atzeres – the final days of the Sukkos holiday

Sheva Brachos – the blessings recited at meals where a bride and groom are present for a week after their wedding; informally: the meals themselves

shidduch – marriage-match

shiur (pl. shiurim) – a Torah-study class

shiva – the seven-day period of mourning for a close relative, when mourners are visited by friends, neighbors and relatives

Shoah – the "Destruction," the Hebrew term used for the Holocaust

shochet – ritual slaughterer of animals for food

shofar – ram's horn, sounded on Rosh Hashana and at the end of the Yom Kippur service

sholom – peace

shtetl – any small pre-war Eastern European town with a Jewish population

siddur – prayer book

siman – an omen or sign

Simchas Torah – the second of Shmini Atzeres' two days, when the completion of the synagogue public reading of the Torah is celebrated

sukkah – "booth," or temporary thatch-roofed dwelling Jews are commanded to us during the holiday of Sukkos

tallis – prayer-shawl

tallis koton – four-cornered undershirt with the fringes prescribed by the Torah hanging from each corner

Talmud – the multi-volume record of the "Oral Law" received at Sinai

Talmud – the recorded Oral Tradition that includes explications of the Torah's laws

Tanach – the Torah (Five Books of Moses), Prophets and Writings

Tata, or **Tateh** – Yiddish for "father"

tefillin – phylacteries, or leather boxes (with verses on parchment inside) and straps worn by Jewish men during morning services (and by some at other times)

Tehillim – Psalms

teitch – the Yiddish translation of Rashi's commentary on the Torah

tereifa – literally: "torn"; an animal that was rendered non-kosher

tzitzis – fringes that hang from the corners of a tallis or tallis koton

vov – the sixth letter of the Hebrew alphabet

yahrtzeit – anniversary of a death, when close relatives traditionally recite the Kaddish-prayer

yeshiva – a school or academy of Torah-study

yingeleh – Yiddish for "little boy"

Yom HaShoah – commemoration of the victims of the Holocaust

Yom Kippur – the Jewish "Day of Atonement," when Jews are commanded to fast, and spend the day in the synagogue reciting special prayers

PHOTOGRAPHS

My parents, surrounded by five of their eight children (counterclockwise, beginning at right): Chaim Meir, Freida Leah, Nachman, Fischel and Tzirel

My paternal grandfather, "Reb Lazer Elya the Melamed"

Right to left: My younger brother Menachem, my sisters Tzirel and Golda, me

My older brother Fischel

The bridge over the Narev at Ruzhan, which we crossed when the Nazis invaded. The photograph was apparently taken by the Germans not long after we crossed the bridge.

FIRE ICE AIR

Our Siberian contingent, in Kavkaz, in 1944:
Upper row, right to left: Yaakov Yeshia Shebrishiner, Moshe Popover
Hellman, Tzvi Tishivitzer Nudel, Chaim Korover, me
Bottom row, right to left: Shlomo Makover Figa, Yaakov Lutzker
Pasternak, Rabbi Nekritz, Yochonon Ostrover Leibeker, Bentzion
Rutger Hirschfeld

My fellow yeshiva students and I (at upper left) in Salzheim

Another photograph from Salzheim (I am at the far left)

PHOTOGRAPHS

A photograph of me taken for the yearbook of Yeshivas Chofetz Chaim (Talmudical Academy) in the early 1950s

My first wedding, on March 13, 1949 at Agudas Achim Anshe Sephard Shul, with Rabbi Yaakov Ruderman presiding

Posing for a snapshot after settling in the United States

The "Vort", or engagement celebration, in 1971, of my daughter Rochel and her husband-to-be Rabbi Meir Zoberman, in our home in Baltimore.
From left to right, facing the camera: Rabbi Dovid Kronglass, Rabbi Yaakov Ruderman, the groom, his father Mr. Shmuel Zoberman (obscured), me, Rabbi Yitzchok Sternhell, Rabbi Mendel Feldman

FIRE ICE AIR

On the ship that brought me from Europe to New York in 1947

Visiting my second cousin, Rabbi Simcha Bunim Shafranovich, of blessed memory, in Jerusalem. He served as the sofer, or scribe, of the Gerer Rebbe

Rabbi Yaakov Yitzchok Ruderman, of blessed memory, reciting a blessing at the wedding of my daughter Rochel and her husband Meir Yechiel Zoberman

With Rabbi Nekritz, of blessed memory, at the wedding

Rabbi Nekritz reading the kesuva at the wedding of my son Avi and his wife Gita

Receiving an honor at the bris of a child born to Iranian Jewish immigrants

With Rabbi Aharon Feldman, the Rosh Yeshiva of Yeshivas Ner Yisroel (far left), and Rabbi Beryl Weisbord, the yeshiva's Mashgiach

With my sons Noach (to my right) and Avi (to my left)

With Rabbi Moshe Heinemann, Rov of Agudath Israel of Baltimore

Participating in a hachnossas sefer Torah — a celebration of the installation of a new Torah scroll — at Yeshivas Chofetz Chaim (behind me is Rabbi Menachem Goldberger).

Teaching a Talmud class in our shul, Adath Yeshurun-Mogen Avrohom Congregation, on Old Court Road

Part of our shul minyan